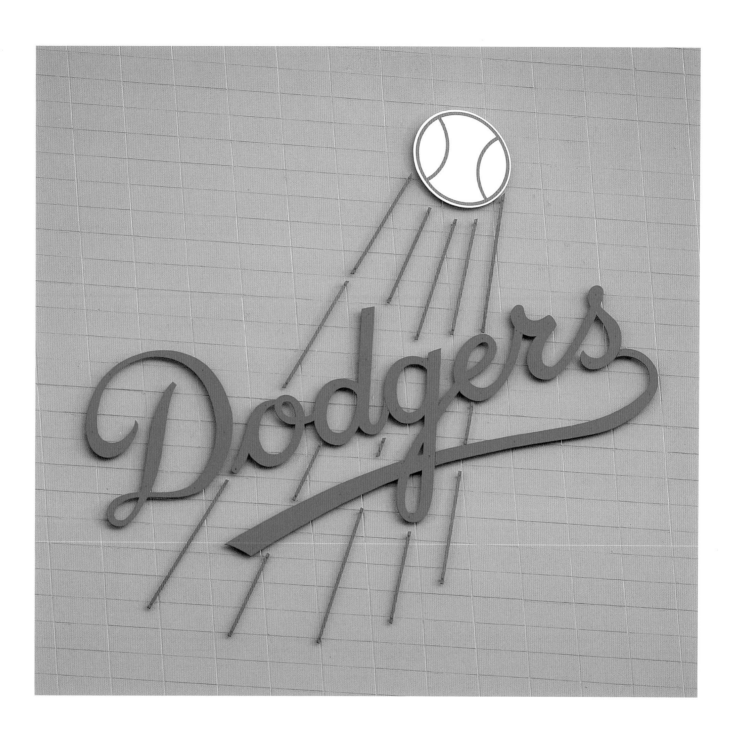

DODGERS
PAST & PRESENT

STEVEN TRAVERS

MVP
BOOKS

To Elizabeth

First published in 2009 by MVP Books, an imprint of MBI Publishing and the Quayside Publishing Group, 400 First Avenue N, Suite 300, Minneapolis, MN 55401 USA

MVP Books titles are also available at discounts in bulk quantity for industrial or sales-promotional use. For details write to Special Sales Manager at Quayside Publishing, 400 First Avenue North, Suite 300, Minneapolis, MN 55401 USA.

Library of Congress Cataloging-in-Publication Data

Travers, Steven.
 Dodgers past & present / Steven Travers. -- 1st ed.
    p. cm.
 Includes bibliographical references and index.
 ISBN 978-0-7603-3527-7 (hb w/ jkt)
1. Los Angeles Dodgers (Baseball team)--History. I. Title.
 GV875.L6T724 2009
 796.357'640979494--dc22
                                    2008038259

Editor: Josh Leventhal
Designer: Lois Stanfield
Cover Design: Elly Rochester

Printed in China

On the front cover: *(top left) 1889 Brooklyn Bridegrooms; (top right) 2007 Los Angeles Dodgers; (bottom) 1955 World Champion Brooklyn Dodgers.*
On the back cover: *(top left) Ebbets Field, Brooklyn, 1954; (top right) Dodger Stadium, Los Angeles, 2003.*
On the title page: *Ebbets Field exterior, circa 1913; (inset) Dodger Stadium at dusk, 1997.*

CONTENTS

PHOTO AND ILLUSTRATION CREDITS

We wish to acknowledge the following for providing the illustrations included in the book. Every effort has been made to locate the copyright holders for materials used, and we apologize for any oversights. Unless otherwise noted, all other images are from the publisher's collection. Individual photographers and collections are listed for photographs when known.

AP/Wide World Photos: p. 9 top left; 9 bottom (Mark J. Terrill); 11 top left; 11 bottom (Ric Francis); 17 top; 17 bottom left; 18; 21 top; 22 bottom; 23 top and bottom; 24; 25 top; 26 top (Rusty Kennedy); 30; 31 top; 32 right; 34 (Robert H. Houston); 35 top (Marcio Jose Sanchez); 36; 37 top; 38 (Edward Kitch); 39 bottom left (Danny Moloshok); 40 bottom (Mark J. Terrill); 41 bottom (Eric Risberg); 43 bottom; 47 bottom; 49 top; 49 bottom (Rick Silva); 51; 53 bottom left (Mark J. Terrill); 55 bottom right; 56; 61 bottom (Richard Drew); 66 top; 67 top (Osamu Honda); 68 (Jack Harris); 69 bottom; 72 left; 73 bottom; 75; 76; 80 top and bottom; 82 (Reed Saxon); 83 left (E. J. Flynn); 83 right (Mark J. Terrill); 85 left (Harry Harris); 85 right; 87 right (Al Behrman); 89 top left; 90; 91 bottom right (Francis Specker); 92 left; 93 top; 94 top (John Lindsay); 95 bottom (Harry Harris); 97 (Kevork Djansezian); 100 bottom; 103 left (Kevork Djansezian); 103 right (Michael A. Mariant); 105 bottom; 107 bottom (Lennox McLendon); 109 bottom right; 111 left (Chris Carlson); 111 right (Al Behrman); 113 bottom left (Wilfredo Lee); 116; 117 top (Ellis R. Bosworth); 117 bottom; 121 top (Dan Grossi); 123 top left (Kevork Djansezian); 123 bottom (Chris Carlson); 124 top (John Lindsay); 127 top (Kevork Djansezian); 129 bottom (Nick Ut); 129 top right (Chris Polk); 131 top left and top right (Richard Lui); 133 top; 133 bottom right (Danny Moloshok); 135 top (Bob Jordan); 135 bottom (Orlin Wagner); 137 left; 139 (Steve Marcus/*Las Vegas Sun*).

Getty Images: p. 1 (Paul Spinelli); 3 (Harry How); 14 top (Leonard Mccombe/Time Life Pictures); 15 bottom (Jon SooHoo/MLB Photos); 17 bottom right (Olen Collection); 19 right (Focus on Sport); 21 (Rogers Photo Archive); 22 top (Curt Gunther); 25 bottom (Robert Riger); 29 left (Barney Stein/Rogers Photo Archive); 29 right (Curt Gunther); 31 bottom (Steve Grayson/WireImage); 35 bottom (Barney Stein/Rogers Photo Archive); 37 bottom (Lisa Blumenfeld); 39 (Jed Jacobsohn/Allsport); 40 top (Art Shay/Time Life Pictures); 41 top (Herb Scharfman/Sports Imagery); 44 top (Barney Stein/Rogers Photo Archive); 44 bottom (Darryl Norenberg/WireImage); 45 top (Rich Pilling/MLB Photos); 45 bottom (Jeff Gross); 47 top (Barney Stein/Rogers Photo Archive); 48 (Focus on Sport); 52 (Jonathan Daniel); 53 top left (Rich Pilling/MLB Photos); 53 bottom right (Michael Zagaris/MLB Photos); 57 left (Rich Pilling/MLB Photos); 57 top right (Louis Requena/MLB Photos); 57 bottom right (Brad Mangin/MLB Photos); 67 bottom (George Rose); 69 top (Mike Nelson/ AFP); 74 top (Robert Riger); 74 bottom right (S Granitz/WireImage); 77 top (Stephen Dunn/Allsport); 77 bottom (Barney Stein/Rogers Photo Archive); 81 (Stephen Dunn); 85 bottom right (Diamond Images); 87 left (Tom Hauck/Allsport); 89 top right; 91 top right (Focus on Sport); 93 bottom (Jeff Gross); 95 top (Tony Linck/Time Life Pictures); 106 left and right (Focus on Sport); 107 top left (Focus on Sport); 107 top right (Stephen Dunn); 110 right (Jed Jacobsohn/Allsport); 121 bottom (Paul Spinelli/MLB Photos); 124 bottom (Francis Miller/Time Life Pictures); 125 top (Andrew D. Bernstein); 125 bottom (Lisa Blumenfeld); 127 bottom (Lisa Blumenfeld); 129 top left (Don Cravens/Time Life Pictures); 131 bottom (Andrew D. Bernstein); 136 (George Silk/Time Life Pictures); 137 right (George Silk/Time Life Pictures); 138 (Andy Hayt).

Library of Congress, Prints and Photographs Division: p. 8 (sketch by J. B. Beale); 10; 16; 27 top; 98 left; 108; 112 left; 130.

Library of Congress, Prints and Photographs Division, George Grantham Bain Collection: p. 20 left; 32 left; 42; 54; 58 left and right; 62 right; 64 left and right; 78 left; 84; 88; 94 bottom; 98 right; 104; 105 top left; 112 right; 113 top left; 115 top right; 128 bottom; 134 top.

National Baseball Hall of Fame Library, Cooperstown, N.Y.: p. 12 bottom; 13 bottom; 15 top; 26 bottom; 43 top; 46 top and bottom; 50 left and right; 53 top right; 55 left; 55 top right; 60; 61 top; 62 left; 65; 70 left and right; 71 left and right; 74 bottom left; 86 top and bottom; 89 bottom; 91 top left; 92 right; 96 right; 97 top; 99 top; 101 bottom; 102 left; 105 top right; 109 top left, top right, and bottom left; 110 left; 113 top right; 113 bottom right (Lou Sauritch); 119 top and bottom; 123 top right; 133 bottom left.

Sauritch, Lou: p. 102 right.

Transcendental Graphics/The Rucker Archive: p. 2; 12 top; 13 top; 27 bottom; 28; 33; 39 top; 59; 72 right; 73 top; 78 right; 79 top and bottom; 96 left; 99 bottom left and bottom right; 100 top; 101 top; 114 top and bottom; 115 top left; 120; 122; 126 bottom left; 128 top; 132 bottom; 134 bottom.

Tringali, Rob Jr.: p. 63 right.

PREFACE

A Voice in the Wilderness

My father and I do not have all things in common, but baseball has been an important connection in our lives, both past and present. I am eternally grateful for this. One of my favorite memories is of family vacations in California's Sierra Mountains. At night we would listen to Vin Scully describe Dodger games on KFI 640 radio. The Dodgers of that era had a bunch of guys whose names were hard to pronounce, and even harder to spell: Grabarkewitz, Sudakis, Lefebvre. Scully eloquently pronounced all their names, and more, without missing a beat. He made the game of baseball sound like the most exciting event imaginable. As we sat around the campfire or in a rickety cabin in the woods, the sounds of Dodger Stadium might as well have emanated from the Roman Colosseum welcoming Caesar from his conquests.

I attended the same suburban California high school that produced USC football coach Pete Carroll and Trojans baseball coach Chad Kreuter. Later, when I was a professional ballplayer, I faced Chad in a high school alumni game. After I mowed down a few of his teammates, Chad laced a single past me. He went on to become the Dodgers' catcher and was behind the plate when Barry Bonds hit his 73rd home run of the 2001 season. I called Chad the "Forrest Gump of baseball" because he always appeared in photos of great baseball moments, like a Nolan Ryan no-hitter, a landmark Rickey Henderson stolen base, and even an incident at Wrigley Field when a fan tried to steal his glove.

My Dodgers connection began early. My high school coach, Al Endriss, had played in the Brooklyn Dodgers' organization in the 1950s. Our practices, training methods, strict discipline, and even uniform styles were modeled on what Coach Endriss learned from Branch Rickey or from teammates like Dick Williams. These methods were successful and resulted in a prep national championship in my senior year. That season, we played Hoover High (the alma mater of Ted Williams) in San Diego. Our unbeaten streak was broken when Hoover's Mike Davis—the same man whom Dennis Eckersley walked to get to Kirk Gibson in the 1988 World Series—tripled against pitcher Buddy Biancalana (who later became the shortstop for the 1985 world champion Royals) to beat us, 6–5.

As a minor leaguer in the Oakland A's organization, I was more a star of the "neon league"—farm-town nightlife, as described by my teammate Dennis Gonsalves—than I was of the California League or any other outfit. I remember the class-A Lodi club arriving at Modesto, and I was struck by the fact that they were the Dodgers. The Twins, the Giants, the Padres—those teams did not seem to impress me as much.

Later, I became embroiled in a "bean ball war" between my club, the Idaho Falls A's, and our Pioneer League opponent, the Lethbridge, Alberta (Canada) Dodgers, in 1982. Their promising shortstop was Mariano Duncan. I recall thinking how incongruous it was that I was "fighting" against a team that I had rooted for since childhood. When I was at USC, my buddies Chris Wildermuth and Terry Marks (who played briefly in the Giants' organization and became president of Coca-Cola North America) went to numerous Dodger games. One time, Chris forced his car into some traffic on Sunset Boulevard and then said, with alarm, "Oh my God. I just cut off Vin Scully." Terry and I turned around, and there was Vinnie. We waved, asking for forgiveness. Like a benevolent priest, Scully waved back and our sins were absolved.

To quote the great man himself, "Pull up a chair. It's time for Dodger baseball."

ACKNOWLEDGMENTS

My thanks go to Josh Leventhal at MVP Books. Thanks to John Horne and Pat Kelly of the Baseball Hall of Fame; Mary at George Brace Photos in Chicago; and the Los Angeles Dodgers. Thanks to Al Endriss, John Rogers, and Bonnie Crosby. Thank you to Vin Scully, and thanks to Lloyd Robinson of Suite A Management in Beverly Hills, California. Thanks to my wonderful daughter, Elizabeth Travers, and my supportive parents. Above all others, my greatest thanks go to my Lord and savior Jesus Christ, the source of all that is decent and true.

INTRODUCTION

Brooklyn Past, LA Present, Dodgers Forever

The story of the Dodgers is the story of baseball and, by extension, the story of America. From the very genesis of the sport, Brooklyn was a hotbed of baseball activity at the amateur, semi-pro, professional, and eventually major league levels. The Dodger franchise also represents the maturation and expansion of the sport into a national and global phenomenon, trailblazing the way for a truly coast-to-coast sport with the move west in 1958. That move made the Dodgers a symbol of a true pioneer in establishing the game's multiethnic, multinational complexion, reflective of the Great American Melting Pot. The team epitomizes the rags-to-riches American dream, transforming from "Dem Bums" to Hollywood glamour boys, from "wait 'til next year" to baseball dynasty. After suffering more than a half-century without a World Series victory, the Dodgers secured more championships over the next half century (six) than any team except the dreaded Yankees.

Throughout their history of triumphs and disappointments, the Dodgers have embodied the intense rivalries and pride of place that has always infused the national pastime. When the Brooklyn Dodgers faced off against the New York Giants, it wasn't just 25 men in each dugout going head to head; it was Brooklyn versus Manhattan. When the Los Angeles Dodgers compete against the San Francisco Giants, it's a clash of cultures from opposite ends of the state—show biz and surfers against fine arts and hippies. When the Dodgers reached the ultimate stage of the World Series to compete against the New York Yankees or Oakland A's—which the franchise has done on 13 occasions in its history—those same passions come to the fore. The players had something to prove not only for the uniforms they wore but for the city or borough they represented.

Regardless of the setting, fans always have identified with "their" Dodgers, who in turn have thrilled the fans of Brooklyn and Los Angeles, New York and California, and America and, indeed, the world, from the likes of Thomas "Oyster" Burns and "Wee Willie" Keeler to Russell Martin and Rafael Furcal.

BASE-BALL MATCH BETWEEN THE "ATHLETICS", OF PHILADELPHIA, PA., AND THE "ATLANTICS," OF BROOKLYN, N. Y., PLAYED AT PHILADELPHIA, OCTOBER 30, 1865.—SKETCHED BY J. B. BEALE.—[SEE PAGE 780.]

Baseball match between the Brooklyn Atlantics and the Philadelphia Athletics, October 1865

Manager Chuck Dressen and his coaches attempt to predict the future during spring training, 1951

Dodgers celebrate winning the division title, September 2008

THE DODGER LEGACY

Among the great sports franchises, the Dodgers rank near the top for tradition and achievement. The conversation inevitably begins with the New York Yankees, the most dominant and successful of all franchises with 26 world titles (8 of them at the Dodgers' expense). But look beyond the raw number of championships—to the Hall of Famers, the MVPs, the all-stars, the pennants, the games won, the pioneers, and the fan support—and it's hard to ignore the Dodgers. This team claims a storied tradition that is, in many ways, greater than any other's.

The Cardinals, Athletics, and Red Sox have amassed more World Series triumphs dating back to 1903 than the Dodgers, but since the integration of major league baseball

Brooklyn Bridegrooms, 1889

in 1947—when it became a truly national game—the Dodgers trail only the Yankees in titles won. The longtime rival Giants haven't tasted the ultimate glory of a championship in more than half a century.

The Baseball Hall of Fame at Cooperstown currently honors 45 individuals who donned a Dodger uniform or sat in the Dodger front office at some point during their careers—a greater number than can be said for the Cardinals, A's, or Red Sox. The Dodgers' nine Cy Young Awards tops all franchises. Eight different Dodger players have won the National League MVP Award; only St. Louis has produced more in the National League. And no franchise, in either league, comes close to the Dodgers' 16 Rookies of the Year.

Off the diamond, the affection that Brooklynites felt for their team is rarely seen in professional sports. Then there is the transcontinental nature of the franchise. The Dodgers have amassed a huge fan base on two coasts and forged baseball's successful migration west, an enormous contribution to the sport. They have set major attendance records, often at a time when the game was hurting for fans.

The Dodgers have played in three iconic ballparks. Ebbets Field was a legendary baseball palace with an intimacy and

character that has inspired a whole generation of "retro-styled" ballparks. Los Angeles Memorial Coliseum had perhaps the most bizarre configuration of any post-1900 baseball facility, yet holds the distinction of hosting the largest baseball crowd in history. Dodger Stadium, now approaching the half-century mark in age, remains a modern baseball shrine that attracts millions of fans every year.

The Dodgers are the team of Jackie Robinson, and in this respect they stand as a ballclub of heroic stature. In addition to breaking down the doors of segregation and injustice, Robinson's arrival in Brooklyn ushered an influx of new talent and greatly impacted how the game was played. The term "National League baseball"—epitomized by aggressive base running and taking the extra base at every opportunity—was perfected by the likes of Robinson, Junior Gilliam, Maury Wills, Davey Lopes, and others wearing Dodger blue.

Perhaps the best summation of what being a Dodger means came from Rick Monday, a star at Santa Monica High School who was acquired by his hometown team in 1977: "Everybody wants to be a Dodger. When you play for the Dodgers, it's more first class than any other team. If you're a Dodger, you know you're a major leaguer."

Brooklyn Dodgers, 1952

Dodger Stadium crowd, 2002

LEAGUES AND TEAMS

Who Are Those Guys?

During baseball's formative years, Brooklyn and Manhattan hosted numerous amateur clubs that competed in a loose confederation. Among Brooklyn's contingent in the 1850s and 1860s were teams known as the Atlantics, Eckfords, and Excelsiors. Those three teams were members, at one time or another, of the National Association of Base Ball Players, which was established in 1857 as the first organized (but still amateur) baseball league. The original 1876 configuration of the National League of Professional Baseball Players—National League for short—did not include any Brooklyn-based teams. But when the new Brooklyn Atlantics joined the American Association in 1884, the lineage of the current Dodgers franchise was born.

Through the closing decades of the nineteenth century, the baseball team from Brooklyn was known alternately as the Atlantics, Grays, Bridegrooms, and Superbas. In the early 1910s, it was branded with the Trolley Dodgers moniker—eventually abbreviated to, simply, Dodgers—because fans had to cross the trolley tracks to reach the ballpark.

The Atlantics finished sixth in association play in its inaugural season of 1884, but by the end of the decade, the team was sitting atop the standings. After capturing its first pennant in 1889,

Brooklyn Atlantics, 1868

the Brooklyn club shifted to the National League for the 1890 campaign and proceeded to win another pennant in that league.

In 1898, the owner of the Baltimore Orioles, which had been the dominant team of the decade, became a part owner of the Brooklyn franchise as well. Over the next two seasons, several of Baltimore's top players, including Wee Willie Keeler and Hughie Jennings, as well as manager Ned Hanlon, were transferred to the Superbas.

Charles Hercules Ebbets, the man who would become the symbol of the franchise, worked his way up from ticket-taker and bookkeeper to becoming a shareholder in 1890. In 1898, he assumed the dual role of team president and manager. Although his turn as field boss was brief (his career managerial record stands at 38–68), Ebbets eventually saved enough money to become the team's principal owner and, in 1913, built a stadium named after himself.

The arrival of Wilbert Robinson as manager in 1914 spurred another name change for the franchise—they were known as the Brooklyn Robins during Robinson's tenure from 1914 to 1931—but only moderate success on the field. Decades of mediocrity were interrupted by two league pennants (1916 and 1920), while the Giants and the Yankees from New York's other boroughs solidified their dominance and Brooklyn's inferiority complex.

Brooklyn Excelsiors, 1859

Left: *Brooklyn Superbas, 1903*

Below: *Brooklyn Robins, 1916*

For two decades following the 1920 pennant, Brooklyn lost more games than it won, but beginning in 1940, the Dodgers established themselves as consistent contenders, winning seven pennants and one World Series title over the club's final 17 seasons in Brooklyn. These teams were known as the "Boys of Summer" by their devoted fans.

In 1958, when Walter O'Malley moved the Dodgers nearly 3,000 miles away to Los Angeles, millions of Brooklynites were heartbroken while millions of baseball-hungry fans in Southern California embraced their new team. Not missing a beat, the Dodgers won three titles during the franchise's first 10 years in Los Angeles. A glorious new stadium opened at Chavez Ravine in 1961, and the capacity crowds were often graced by Hollywood A-listers.

In 1962, the arrival of an expansion team in Queens, New York, not only provided a natural extension for the old Brooklyn fan base, but the addition of the Mets, Houston Astros, Montreal Expos, and San Diego Padres during the 1960s also led to the realignment of the league into two divisions. In 1969, the Los Angeles Dodgers became part of the National League's West Division.

Los Angeles Dodgers, Opening Day 1958

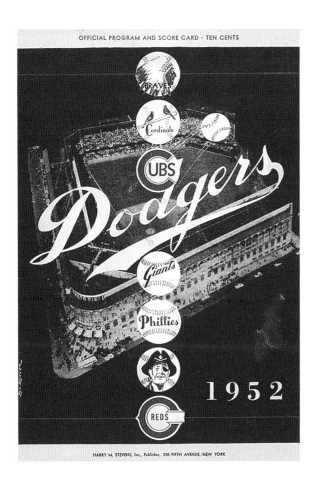

Although overshadowed by Cincinnati's "Big Red Machine" for much of the decade, the Dodgers held their own as an elite team in the West and made three trips to the Fall Classic during the 1970s. Los Angeles' two World Series appearances in the 1980s netted two championships, but the 1988 title was followed by two decades (and counting) without another pennant.

With expansion into two new major league cities, a third division was added to each league in 1994. The Dodgers said goodbye to their longtime division rivals from Atlanta, which the commissioner's office finally recognized as part of the eastern seaboard. The Reds and Astros took off for the newly created Central Division, while the revamped West Division held on to the National League's three California clubs and added a new team from the rarified air of Colorado. The creation of the Arizona Diamondbacks (along with the Tampa Bay Devil Rays) in 1998 brought the number of major league teams to 30 and introduced a new rival to the Dodgers' midst.

The Dodgers were the only members of the NL West not to reach the World Series during the first decade of the five-team division—as Los Angeles managed two division crowns and one wild-card spot from 1998 to 2008—but the intensity of intra-division rivalries, the passion of faithful fans, and the glory of Dodger Blue remain strong after more than 125 years of play, and more than half a century in Los Angeles.

Brooklyn Dodgers, 1955

Los Angeles Dodgers, 2007

DODGER DYNASTIES

Reaching the Top

etween 1860 and 1870, the baseball team from Brooklyn won five "national championships," but that iteration of the Atlantics has no direct link to the later National League franchise. The ballclub that would trace its development to the Dodgers had some great teams in the franchise's early years of the 1880s and 1890s. The 93–44 campaign in 1889, under manager Bill McGunnigle, was the first of two consecutive titles for the team in two different leagues—first in the American Association and then, in 1890, the National League.

Hall of Fame manager Ned Hanlon led Brooklyn to consecutive pennants a decade later, setting the franchise's best single-season mark in 1899 (101–47, .682). Under Wilbert "Uncle Robbie" Robinson, the Brooklyn club won pennants in 1916 and 1920 but lost in both World Series appearances. (Those two first-place finishes were separated by three losing seasons.) Boasting future Hall of Famers in Zack Wheat, Rube Marquard, and

Burleigh Grimes, Uncle Robbie's teams were good, but not quite a dynasty.

The Dodger teams of the mid-twentieth century had the talent to be dynasties. Between 1940 and 1956, they nabbed seven National League pennants and finished below third place in the standings only once. Brooklyn went down to the wire against St. Louis in 1942 and 1946, then against Philadelphia in 1950, and famously fell victim to Bobby Thomson's "shot heard 'round the world" in 1951. The 1949 team saw Jackie Robinson win the Most Valuable Player award, Don Newcombe earn Rookie of the Year honors, and Duke Snider, Gil Hodges, Carl Furillo, Pee Wee Reese, and Roy Campanella come into their own as stars, but the season ended with yet another October loss. Although Brooklyn did challenge the Yankees in several thrilling World Series contests, and ultimately beat them in 1955, Dodger fans saw more disappointment than jubilation in the 1940s and 1950s.

Brooklyn Atlantics, 1864

Brooklyn Superbas, 1900

Duke Snider and Don Newcombe celebrate the 1955 championship

Duke Snider, Jackie Robinson, and Pee Wee Reese hold the 1952 league champion ceremonial bat

1963 World Champion Los Angeles Dodgers

The Dodgers' true dynasty is the period in Los Angeles between 1959 and 1966. The team captured three world championships and four league pennants, and nearly had a fifth in 1962. A head-to-head matchup with their old nemesis from the Bronx in the 1963 World Series saw complete domination by Los Angeles and a four-game sweep. Take away the subpar 80–82 outing in 1964, and the Dodgers won an average of 98 games from 1962 to 1966.

The 1962 club, winners of 102 games, might have been the best of this period. Outside of the 1955 championship team, the 1962 club was perhaps the best of all time. A heartbreaking loss to their rivals from San Francisco in a three-game playoff cut the World Series dream short. Strong competition for the honor of best Dodgers team also comes from the 1951 club, which similarly blew a pennant at the hands of the Giants. The 1953 Brooklyn team won more regular-season games (105) than any Dodger team in history, but lost a hard-fought, seven-game World Series to the Yankees.

The 1966 squad had the look of a dynasty as it won an intense pennant race against stiff competition from San Francisco and Pittsburgh. Although the offense didn't put a lot of runs on the board, the Dodgers' speed, defense, and pitching were good enough for the team's fourth pennant since coming west. The veteran club seemed poised to dispose of the "Baby Birds" of Baltimore in the World Series, but the dynasty-in-the-making from Baltimore completely silenced the Dodger bats in a surprise sweep.

Legendary hurlers Sandy Koufax and Don Drysdale were gone by the end of the 1960s, but the Dodgers re-emerged as consistent contenders throughout the 1970s. They finished first or

Game program, 1978 NLCS, showing Los Angeles pennants

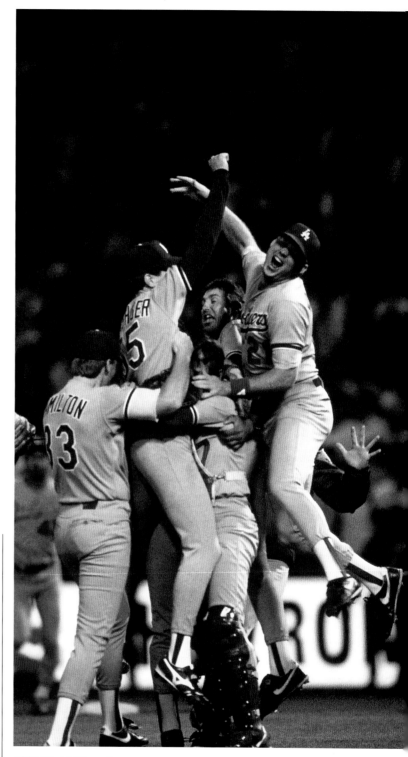

1988 World Champions

second in the division every year from 1970 to 1978, including five 90-plus-win seasons. Although they never won it all, players and fans could take some consolation in the knowledge that the teams they lost to, both in their own division and in the World Series, included some of the greatest teams ever assembled: the Oakland A's in 1974, the Yankees in 1977 and 1978, and the Cincinnati Reds five times in the decade.

The 1980s was a strange decade for Los Angeles: four division crowns and four sub-.500 seasons, bookended by two world titles. Most of the stars from the 1981 champs were gone or had limited roles in the 1988 victory. The Dodgers were heavy underdogs heading into the 1988 postseason, first against the Mets in the League Championship Series and then against Oakland in the World Series. The A's thought they were among the all-time greats. Kirk Gibson, Orel Hershiser, Mickey Hatcher, and the rest of the Dodgers had something else to say about that—and secured the franchise's sixth world championship.

THE WORLD SERIES
It's What They Play For

The first modern World Series was played in 1903 between the Boston Pilgrims and Pittsburgh Pirates, but the Brooklyn Bridegrooms participated in a precursor championship series in the previous century. As champions of the American Association in 1889, Brooklyn played a nine-game postseason exhibition against the National League–champion New York Giants and won, six games to three. The following year, having switched leagues,

1941 World Series program cover

Brooklyn manager Wilbert Robinson and Boston manager Bill Carrigan, 1916 World Series

the Bridegrooms represented the NL against the AA-champion Louisville Colonels in a seven-game competition that ended inconclusively, with three wins for each side and one tie.

Since 1903, the Dodgers' have appeared in baseball's Fall Classic more times (18) than any other National League club. Those series have had no shortage of memorable moments. Brooklyn's first trip to the World Series came in 1916 and featured a classic 14-inning pitchers' duel in Game Two. Brooklyn pitcher Sherry Smith and a young lefty named Babe Ruth both went the distance in Boston's 2–1 marathon win. The Red Sox took the series in five games. Four years later, the Brooklyn Robins fell victim to an unprecedented unassisted triple play by Bill Wambsganss of the

Cleveland Indians in Game Five. The Indians clinched the best-of-nine 1920 series in seven games.

Brooklyn would go another two decades before returning to the Fall Classic. When they finally got there, on the backs of a 100–54 record in 1941, the Dodgers faced a formidable New York Yankees team. The "Bronx Bombers" welcomed Leo Durocher's Dodgers to the big stage with a five-game thumping. Once again, a Brooklyn blunder would enter the annals of baseball history, as catcher Mickey Owen's passed ball sparked a Yankee rally in the ninth inning of Game Four.

The golden age of the Dodgers-Yankees rivalry revolves around the six Subway Series that took place between 1947 and 1956. The '47 Fall Classic had more than its share of drama, highlighted (for Dodger fans) by Cookie Lavagetto's two-run pinch-hit double in the ninth inning of Game Four. The hit broke up New York pitcher Bill Bevens' no-hitter and won the game for Brooklyn. Leftfielder Al Gionfriddo preserved a Game Six win with a superb catch of a long drive by Joe DiMaggio, causing the usually stoic "Yankee Clipper" to kick at the base path in frustration. Brooklyn couldn't carry the momentum into Game Seven, however, and the Yankees overcame the upstart Dodgers, 5–2, at Yankee Stadium.

Al Gionfriddo robs Joe DiMaggio, Game Six, 1947 World Series

Yankee visitor jokes with Leo Durocher in Dodgers dugout, 1941 World Series

David Halberstam called 1949 the best year in baseball history, but after an intense pennant race with St. Louis, Brooklyn's season came to a disappointing end in the World Series. Aside from a 1–0 win in Game Two, the Dodgers never held the lead against Casey Stengel's Yankees in any inning of the five-game series. Dodger pitcher Preacher Roe's complete-game shutout in the second game was the lone bright spot for "Dem Bums."

It was the same old story for the Dodgers in 1952 and 1953. Brooklyn and New York alternated wins through the first six games of the 1952 series, but the pattern was broken when the Yanks captured the clinching game at Ebbets Field. Although Duke Snider clubbed four home runs in the series, and Joe Black made history as the first African-American pitcher to win a World Series game, Brooklyn once again fell short. Billy Martin's running catch of Jackie Robinson's pop-up in the seventh inning of the final game killed a Brooklyn rally and proved to be the pivotal moment.

Jackie Robinson, Preacher Roe, and Gil Hodges enjoy their lone win of the 1949 World Series

Duke Snider homers at Ebbets Field, Game One, 1952 World Series

1955 World Champion Brooklyn Dodgers

In 1953, Martin undid Brooklyn again—this time with his bat, as he collected 12 hits in the six-game Yankee triumph. As a team, the Dodgers outhit the Yankees 64 to 56, but they couldn't get the runs across the plate. The highlight for Brooklyn was Carl Erskine's record-setting 14-strikeout performance in the Game Three win.

After 1955, nobody called them Bums again. The Dodgers battled back after losing the first two games of the World Series to win the next three at home. They lost Game Six in Yankee Stadium, but then mounted an improbable victory in the Bronx in the deciding game. Series MVP Johnny Podres was masterful in Game Seven, shutting out the Bombers for his second win of the series. Sandy Amoros' spectacular catch of Yogi Berra's opposite-field drive down the line, followed by Pee Wee Reese's relay to double-up Gil McDougald at first base, helped to preserve the 2–0 lead. Snider again collected four homers in the series to become the only player ever to accomplish the feat twice. At long last, the Dodgers had reached the Promised Land.

A year later, the Yankees got their revenge and won another seven-game series, which was most noteworthy for Don Larsen's perfect game.

Carl Erskine congratulated by teammates, Game Three, 1953 World Series

Record crowd at Los Angeles Coliseum, Game Five, 1959 World Series

In 1958—the team's first year in Los Angeles—the Dodgers posted their first losing season in more than a decade, but the postseason hiatus didn't last long. They were back on top in 1959, this time to face the Chicago White Sox. With many new faces compared to the 1955 champs, the Dodgers bounced back from an 11–0 thrashing at Comiskey Park in the opener to win the series in six games. The series drew record attendance, including crowds of 92,000-plus at the three games in the massive Los Angeles Coliseum.

As the "Boys of Summer" gave way to a new generation of all-stars, the Dodgers reached the Fall Classic three times

in four years in the 1960s. In 1963, they reunited with their old nemeses from the Bronx, and what followed was nothing short of astonishing. With much pregame build-up, the opener pitted two Hall of Fame lefties against each other: Sandy Koufax vs. Whitey Ford. Los Angeles' southpaw struck out the side in the first inning and went on to set a new postseason record with 15 strikeouts for the game. The Dodger hitters, meanwhile, chipped away at Ford. LA prevailed, 5–2. The hero of 1955, Johnny Podres, won Game Two, and then Don Drysdale bested Jim Bouton in a 1–0 thriller at Dodger Stadium in the third game. In Game Four, Koufax struck out "only" eight batters, outdueled Ford 2–1, and it was all over. The Dodger staff held the Bombers to a total of four runs in the four-game sweep.

In 1965 and 1966, the veteran, postseason-tested Dodgers faced newcomers to the October stage. Against Minnesota in 1965, it looked bleak after the heavy-hitting Twins took the first two games against Los Angeles' duo of aces. Drysdale got the Game One start when Koufax opted not to pitch on the Jewish holiday of Yom Kippur, but Drysdale didn't last beyond the third inning. Koufax earned the loss in Game Two. Claude Osteen got LA back on track with a shutout in Game Three, and after that it was the "Don and Sandy Show." In the deciding seventh game, manager Walter Alston opted to go with Koufax on three days' rest, rather than Drysdale on four days, and the lefty's 10-strikeout, 3-hitter made Alston look like a genius.

With Koufax and Drysdale rested and ready to go in 1966, the Dodgers took on the young and unproven Baltimore Orioles. The Dodgers' dominant pitching was on display, and Baltimore could not hit a lick. But the "hitless wonders" from Los Angeles set new records of ineptitude at the plate, scoring a total of just two runs in the four-game sweep.

Koufax fires one in, Game Seven, 1965 World Series

Sandy Koufax pitches to Roger Maris, Game One, 1963 World Series

The Dodgers of the 1970s played in three World Series, and all three ended in disappointment. The 1974 squad fell to a great Oakland A's team in five games, losing three of the games by just one run. Then, in 1977, the Yankees' "Mr. October," Reggie Jackson, was awesome in New York's six-game win. A year later, those same Yankees overcame Los Angeles' two-games-to-none lead to wrap up another championship at the Dodgers' expense.

Revenge came in 1981, when the Yankees won the first two games only to lose the next four. Rookie Fernando Valenzuela stemmed the Yankee tide with his complete-game win in Game Three at Dodger Stadium. Ron Cey, Pedro Guerrero, and Steve Yeager drove in 17 of the team's 26 runs to share in the first three-way series MVP award.

The story in 1988 can be summed up with two names: Kirk Gibson and Orel Hershiser. After Gibson's *The Natural*-esque pinch-hit homer against Dennis Eckersley secured the 5–4 Game One victory, announcer Jack Buck said, "I don't believe what I just saw." This contrasted with Vin Scully's more subdued description on the radio: "It's outta here." It was Gibson's only at-bat of the series. Hershiser stepped up and hurled a complete-game shutout in the second contest and then sealed the upset victory over the imposing Oakland A's with another complete-game triumph in Game Five, bringing the Dodger franchise its sixth world championship.

Kirk Gibson, 1988 World Series

General manager Al Campanis, baseball commissioner Bowie Kuhn, owner Peter O'Malley, and manager Tommy Lasorda hoist the 1981 World Series trophy

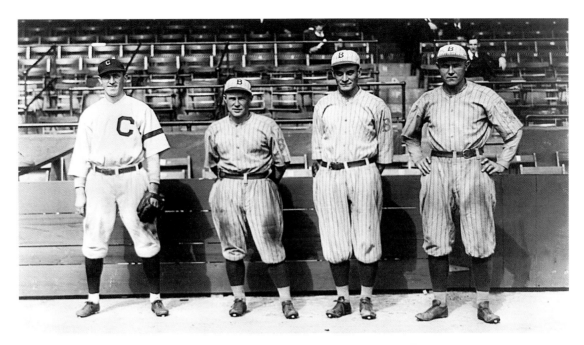

Cleveland's Bill Wambsganss with Pete Kilduff, Clarence Mitchell, and Otto Miller, 1920

WAIT 'TIL NEXT YEAR

Dodger Disappointments

Despite 22 league pennants and 6 World Series titles, the Dodger legacy is often associated more with disappointment than triumph. Dodger fans had to wait more than 50 years before they could celebrate a World Series win, and it wasn't for lack of opportunity. Their seven appearances in the Fall Classics held from 1903 to 1953 trailed only the Cubs, Cardinals, and Giants in the National League—but while those three teams accounted for 13 world titles between them, the Dodgers posted an 0–7 record in October during that half century. Brooklyn went two full decades without a pennant (1921–1940), a stretch of futility the team is at risk of surpassing in the aftermath of the 1988 championship.

Even in years when the team made it to the World Series, Brooklyn's most vivid memories were typically of disaster, defeat, or demoralization. Such was the case in the 1920 World Series, when the Cleveland Indians not only beat the Brooklyn Robins five games to two but embarrassed them with the only unassisted triple play in the history of postseason baseball. With Brooklyn's Pete Kilduff and Otto Miller on base and running with the hit,

Clarence Mitchell drove a liner that was snagged by Cleveland second baseman Bill Wambsganss. He ran to second base, doubled up Kilduff, then tagged Miller, who ran right into the third out.

The Brooklyn Bum

Another classic Dodger lowlight came during the 1941 World Series. Brooklyn trailed New York two games to one but were on the verge of tying the series in Game Four. Holding a 4–3 lead in the top of the ninth, Dodger spitball artist Hugh Casey retired the first two Yankee batters. With the fans in a frenzy, Casey threw two strikes to Tommy Henrich and then induced him to swing and miss for strike three—but the ball skidded away from catcher Mickey Owen. According to the *New York Herald-Tribune*, Owen went after the ball "in a vivid imitation of a man changing a tire, grabbing monkey wrenches, screwdrivers, inner tubes, and a jack, and he couldn't find any of them." Henrich reached first base safely, and the Yankees rallied to win the game 7–4. "I lost a lot of ballgames in some funny ways," said Casey, "but this is the first time I ever lost a game by striking out a man." The great sportswriter Red Smith wrote, "Nowhere else in this broad, untidy universe, not in Bedlam or in Babel nor in the remotest psychopathic ward nor the sleaziest padded cell . . . could a man win a World Series game by striking out."

Nearly ten years to the day later came the Titanic of Dodger disasters. During the deciding third game of the 1951 playoff

Mickey Owen chasing passed ball as Tommy Henrich runs to first, 1941 World Series

Ralph Branca, October 3, 1951

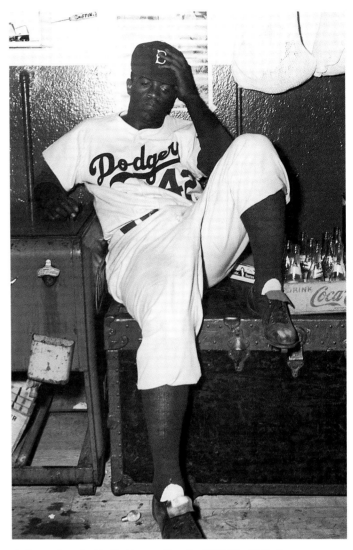

A despondent Jackie Robinson after the 1952 World Series

between the Dodgers and the Giants, New York's Bobby Thomson tommy-hawked Ralph Branca's high strike and drove a low liner into the Polo Grounds' short leftfield bleachers for a three-run home run and a 5–4 victory. The Giants won the pennant.

The following year, the Dodgers again led the way through most of the season, and history threatened to repeat itself when Brooklyn slumped and New York had a late-season charge. Former Dodger and current Giants manager Leo Durocher proclaimed that, if the Giants were to win again, "there'll be 100,000 suicides in Brooklyn." This time, the Dodgers held off and won the pennant, but in the World Series, star slugger Gil Hodges posted one of the

worst performances in postseason history, going 0-for-21 as the Bums failed to beat the Yanks in the Series . . . again.

Transplanted to the West Coast, the Dodgers went from Bums to brilliant seemingly overnight, winning three World Series in three trips between 1959 and 1965. The darkest cloud during that stretch was the 1962 season, when the Dodgers again lost a pennant to the Giants after the two teams finished the regular season with identical records. Although there was no "shot heard 'round the world," Los Angeles was left with the unpleasant taste of failing to make the World Series despite winning 102 games— the franchise's highest West Coast win total.

Willie Davis commits an error, 1966 World Series

In 1966, the ghosts of disasters past seemed to find their way to sunny California again. Los Angeles native Willie Davis was one of the finest centerfielders of his era. The reputation of his defensive acumen is diminished only because he had to compete with Willie Mays and Roberto Clemente for Gold Glove Awards, but the Dodgers were more than happy to have Davis in the field six days of the week and twice on Sunday. Any day, that is, but Game Two of the 1966 World Series.

As Sandy Koufax engaged in a shutout duel with Baltimore's Jim Palmer, Davis proceeded to twice lose balls in Los Angeles' "fierce, smog-glazed sun," according to Roger Angell in *The*

Summer Game. The second error he compounded with "an angry little league heave into the Dodger dugout," making it a record three errors in one inning for Davis. Overall, six Dodger errors undid Koufax's efforts in the 6–0 loss. In Game Four at Baltimore's Memorial Stadium, Davis made one of the greatest catches in World Series history when he robbed Boog Powell of a homer, but it seemed merely to mock his previous blunders, and the Dodgers went down in an easy sweep.

As had been the case in the 1940s and 1950s, the Dodgers of the 1970s had plenty of talent but had the misfortune of running up against all-time dynasties. They lost two World Series to their old rivals from New York, the Yankees. In 1978, the Dodgers became the first team to lose a series in six games after winning the first two.

Although they failed to win the World Series during the 1970s, the Dodgers almost always seemed to make the right moves. As free agency took hold and many clubs spent wildly, the Dodgers, even with their great wealth, were more judicious and still experienced on-field success.

In the 1990s, the wheels started to come off. With billionaire Rupert Murdoch in charge, the club started to spend big—and foolishly. After letting catcher Mike Piazza walk away to seek his fortunes elsewhere, the Dodger management offered $105 million and a private plane to free-agent Kevin Brown. The right-handed hurler had been a star in Texas and San Diego and boasted a nasty, sinking fastball, but he was no Christy Mathewson or Nolan Ryan. He posted an 18–9 record in 1999 and led the league in ERA in 2000, but the Dodgers failed to make the playoffs during Brown's five-year stay.

The year after Brown left, the Dodgers won their first post–Tommy Lasorda division title. The team led the West for all but 23 days of the season, only to lose to the St. Louis Cardinals in the 2004 League Division Series. Two years later, Los Angeles launched a seven-game winning streak to close the season and earn the Wild Card spot, but then dropped three straight games to the Mets in the playoffs.

Tommy Lasorda consoles Steve Garvey after the 1977 World Series

Los Angeles Dodgers, Game Four, 2004 League Division Series

THE DODGER-GIANT RIVALRY

Blood Feud

For manager John McGraw and the rest of the New York Giants of the early 1900s, Brooklyn's teams were not worthy of the term "rival." In New York's 10 pennant seasons under McGraw, Brooklyn never finished anywhere near the top of the standings, except in 1924 when a 15-game winning streak by the Robins in August and September gave the Giants a run for their money.

In 1934, Giants player-manager Bill Terry was asked about the effect that a season-ending series with Brooklyn might have on his club's pennant race with St. Louis.

"Brooklyn?" scoffed Terry. "Are they still in the league?"

Although Brooklyn's 71–81 record kept them far out of the 1934 pennant race, the Dodgers did their part to deny the Giants a pennant by defeating them in the final two games of the season, allowing St. Louis to clinch first place.

The balance of power shifted in the 1940s, with Brooklyn winning three pennants while New York won none. Then came 1951. In early August of that year, the Giants were a full 13 games behind the Dodgers in the standings. New York then put together one of the greatest rallies in baseball history, winning 37 of the season's final 44 games. The Giants won their last game to temporarily move ahead of Brooklyn, but the Dodgers beat the Phillies in their final game to finish with an identical record as their cross-city nemeses. The pennant would be decided by a best-of-three-game playoff series. The teams split the first two games, and the Giants were trailing 4–1 in the bottom of the ninth inning

Giants manager John McGraw and Brooklyn manager Wilbert Robinson, 1915

Los Angeles manager Walter Alston, October 3, 1962

of the third game at the Polo Grounds. Then, the Giants staged a legendary comeback, capped by Bobby Thomson's game-winning home-run off of Ralph Branca—baseball's "shot heard 'round the world." (Years later, it was revealed that the Giants were stealing the Dodgers' signs through a scoreboard lookout, which only added to Dodger bitterness.)

In 1962, with both teams relocated in California, history repeated itself. After defeating the Giants on the last game before the All-Star Break, the Dodgers assumed first place and held onto it for the next 85 days. But a four-game lead on September 22

quickly vanished, as the Dodgers lost six games in the final week of the season while the Giants won five of their last seven. Los Angeles' tailspin forced another playoff between the two teams, as both finished with 101–61 records. As it had been 11 years earlier, the Giants took the first game of the playoff and the Dodgers took game two. The Giants' 6–4 win on October 3 wrapped up the pennant and sparked a major meltdown in the Dodgers' clubhouse, with massive amounts of alcohol consumption and furniture-tossing, while manager Walt Alston barricaded himself in his office.

Jackie Robinson (42) watches the Giants celebrate Bobby Thomson's "shot heard 'round the world," October 3, 1951

In 1965, the rivalry took its ugliest turn. On August 22, in the midst of another intense pennant race, the Dodgers and Giants faced off in the final game of a four-game series at Candlestick Park in San Francisco. Aces Sandy Koufax and Juan Marichal were the starters. When Marichal—who had sent two Dodger batters to the deck with brush-back pitches earlier in the game—stepped to the plate, Dodger catcher John Roseboro buzzed Marichal's ear on a throw back to the mound. (Roseboro had asked Koufax to bean Marichal, but Koufax refused.) Marichal turned and clubbed the catcher over the head with his bat. The benches cleared and a brawl ensued. Marichal was ejected and later received an eight-game suspension, while Roseboro earned 14 stitches to close up his head wound. The Dodgers lost the game, and although there was no more violence, the teams battled in the standings for the remainder of the season.

After the Giants reeled off 14 straight wins in September to take a 4½-game lead, it looked as if the Dodgers might be headed for another historic collapse. (They had held first place for all but five days between May 1 and September 1.) But a 13-game winning streak catapulted the Dodgers back into the top spot in the closing week of the season.

Another down-to-the-wire race for the pennant followed in 1966, and again Los Angeles wrapped it up in the season's final week. Five years later, the Giants eked out a division title despite a late-season surge by the Dodgers. In 1982, the Dodgers and Giants were engaged in a three-way struggle with Atlanta, and a game-winning home run by San Francisco's Joe Morgan in the season's final game provided the death blow to Los Angeles' postseason hopes.

In more recent years, the two teams generally have not vied for first place at the same time, but that hasn't lessened either team's desire to defeat the other. The Giants denied the Dodgers a chance at a division title in 1991 by beating them in two out of three games in the final weekend. In 1993, a 12–1 thrashing by the Dodgers in the last game of the season left the Giants one game back of the first-place Braves. The 1997 West Division lead flipped back and forth between the two throughout August and September, but a disappointing 10–14 finish for the Dodgers sent the Giants to the postseason.

With Barry Bonds blasting home-run records, the Giants took the upper hand in the rivalry in the early 2000s. Los Angeles got some measure of revenge in 2004 when, in the second-to-last game of the season, Steve Finley's ninth-inning grand slam at Dodger Stadium knocked the Giants out of the playoffs and clinched a postseason berth for the Dodgers.

During the teams' East Coast lives, the Giants ruled, with five World Series triumphs compared to Brooklyn's one. But since heading west in 1958, San Francisco has not managed any world titles while the Dodgers have surpassed the Giants by adding five more trophies to the championship shelf. The Dodgers, once a joke in the eyes of Giants stalwarts like John McGraw and Bill Terry, have established themselves as the greater of the two franchises.

Juan Marichal (#27) attacking Johnny Roseboro, August 22, 1965

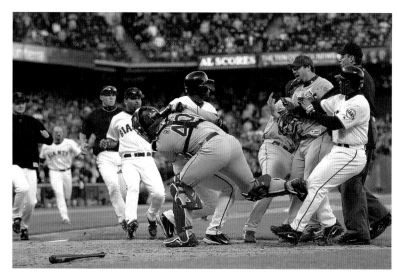

Dodgers-Giants brawl, June 2004

Dodgers-Giants brawl, April 1953

THE DODGER-YANKEE RIVALRY
Going Coastal

The first time the Brooklyn Dodgers and New York Yankees met on the baseball diamond, it was 1913, and Brooklyn notched a 3–2 win at Ebbets Field in an exhibition game. Similar contests were held in subsequent years, but the two franchises didn't play each other in a game that mattered until 1941, when Brooklyn finally shed its also-ran identity and stood up to face the Yankees in the Fall Classic. At the helm for the Dodgers was Leo Durocher, who began his playing career as a Yankee in the 1920s but was drummed out of the corps for being un-Yankee-like. Although the presence of "Leo the Lip" added to the tension, Mickey Owen's infamous passed ball in the 1941 series came to symbolize what would be years of letdowns in encounters with the Bronx Bombers.

Even as the personnel in pinstripes changed over the years— Joe DiMaggio giving way to Mickey Mantle, Bill Dickey to Yogi Berra, Joe McCarthy to Casey Stengel—the results were the same.

In 1947, 1949, 1952, and 1953, Brooklyn met New York in the World Series. Sometimes the series went seven games, sometimes five or six games (never a sweep), but always with the same team celebrating when it was over.

In 1953, the Dodgers arrived in October with 105 regular-season wins. People called them the best National League team of all time. No matter: the Yankees won again. On one occasion, Mickey Mantle came to bat and was heckled by the Ebbets Field faithful. He responded with a monster homer that bounced, rattled, and dented the cars of those fans outside the ballpark.

In 1955, "next year" arrived. After losing the first two games in the series, Walter Alston's Dodgers won four of the next five to prevail over Stengel's Yankees. Johnny Podres led the way from the mound, Sandy Amoros provided heroics with the glove, and Gil Hodges drove in both Dodger runs. Brooklynites celebrated through the night.

Lou Gehrig at the plate in a Yankees-Dodgers exhibition at Norfolk, Virginia, April 13, 1939

The "Boys of Summer" again ruled the National League roost in 1956, but that year's World Series was the same old story, as the Yanks won in seven games. The ghosts of Brooklyn past were exorcised in 1963 when Koufax, Drysdale, and company dominated in a four-game sweep—the first such humiliation for the Yankees in 25 World Series appearances since 1922. Vin Scully calls the 1963 win the highlight of all Dodger highlights.

Just as the Yankees redeemed their 1955 loss with a win the very next year, redemption too came for the 1963 loss, albeit many years later. In 1977, Reggie Jackson belted five home runs—each of which made Dodgers' manager Tommy Lasorda "sick to my stomach"—and helped bring George Steinbrenner his first championship. A year later, Jackson and the Yankees did it again, clinching the series at Dodger Stadium in Game Six.

To date, the last word in the rivalry that has spanned two coasts lies with the Dodgers, who in 1981 won a third World Series victory against the great Yankee franchise.

Interleague play was introduced in 1997, but the schedule-makers did not arrange a meeting between the old rivals from Los Angeles and New York until 2004. The Dodgers won two out of three at home in front of capacity crowds.

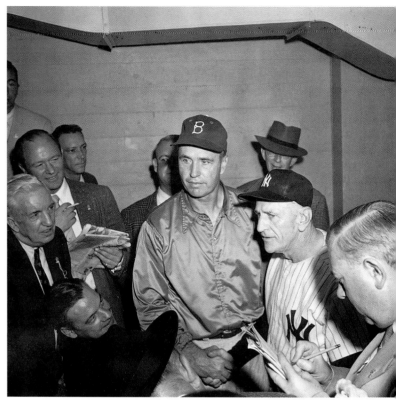

Casey Stengel congratulates Walter Alston after 1955 World Series

Dodgers vs. Yankees at Dodger Stadium, June 2004

OTHER RIVALS

Cardinals and Angels and Reds, Oh My!

With a history that goes back more than a century, the Dodger franchise has squabbled with teams from most National League cities and some American League ones, too. At various times, Dodger enemy number one has resided in St. Louis, Cincinnati, Milwaukee, Atlanta, San Diego, and elsewhere.

When Brooklyn emerged as consistent contenders, the team's most common foil was the St. Louis Cardinals, who won four pennants to the Dodgers' three during the 1940s. In 1946, it took a best-of-three playoff series to decide the league champ after both teams finished with a record of 96–58—the first time in major league history that two teams finished atop the standings with identical records. The introduction of divisional play in 1969 put some distance between the East Division Cardinals and West Division Dodgers, but the two met in a dramatic League Championship Series in 1985 that ended with St. Louis winning it in the final inning of Game Six. The teams met again in 2004 in the League Division Series, and again St. Louis took the series en route to a pennant. Vin Scully has commented that no matter how many times the Cardinals and Dodgers play each other, the all-time record always hovers around .500.

The strong Cincinnati Reds teams of the early 1940s were in the mix with Brooklyn and St. Louis, but Cincinnati's role as top Dodger rival hit its prime when the Big Red Machine of Johnny Bench, Pete Rose, and Joe Morgan was racking up titles in the 1970s. The Dodgers and Reds were one and two in the West Division every season from 1973 through 1978—with three first-place finishes for each—as well as in 1970. In 1973, the Dodgers held the division lead from mid-June through early September, but a losing record for the final month opened the door for the Reds.

The Milwaukee Braves broke the Dodgers' stranglehold on the National League pennant in the 1950s when they won back-to-back titles in 1957 and 1958. In 1959, the teams finished in a tie for first and faced off in a playoff for the league crown. The Dodgers clinched it with a 12-inning triumph in Game Two. The creation of divisions in 1969 put the now-Atlanta Braves with Los Angeles in the West. In 1982, Atlanta grabbed its first division title since 1969 when a late-September swoon by the Dodgers allowed the Braves to swoop in. A similar outcome came in 1991 when the Dodgers lost the lead on the final weekend after leading the division nearly uninterrupted since mid-May.

The addition of an expansion team in San Diego in 1969 gave the Dodgers their nearest National League competitor since coming west. The rivalry with the Padres has a Southern California flavor and can be as intense as any. In the 1980s, Padre players started the practice of high-fiving each other when they scored against the Dodgers, which caused much consternation with Tommy Lasorda's team. After longtime first baseman Steve Garvey departed Los Angeles for San Diego, he helped the Padres shed their second-class status by leading them to a pennant in 1984. San Diego won another pennant in 1998, and to date, the Dodgers have gone longer than any other California team without a trip to the World Series.

Dodger catcher Mickey Owen (10) attacks Cardinal catcher Walker Cooper, igniting a brawl, August 1943

Brooklyn Dodgers and Milwaukee Braves brawl, 1957

Dodger Matt Kemp scuffles with Yorvit Torrealba of the division rival Colorado Rockies, June 2008

Dodgers and Padres brawl, June 1993

Dodger owner Walter O'Malley (left) with Angels owner Gene Autry, early 1960s

Dodgers and Angels brawl in an interleague game, July 1997

When the Los Angeles Angels were first established as an American League expansion team in 1961, they played at Wrigley Field on Avalon Boulevard, but after Dodger Stadium was unveiled in 1962, the Angels became tenants of Walter O'Malley and the Dodgers. It was not a happy relationship. The Angels' ticket offices were placed in a hard-to-find area outside the stadium. Their clubhouse was crowded and offered none of the amenities the Dodgers enjoyed. O'Malley penuriously charged the Angels for towels, toilet paper, soap, and anything else he could get away with. He was forever concerned about the new team on the block cutting into his fan base.

Although some of the tension was alleviated after the Angels moved to Orange County, the two teams constantly warred over fan and media attention. A preseason "freeway series" exhibition was established, which continued even after the institution of interleague competition. The introduction of official games between the two in the 1990s heated up the intensity. The Dodgers won all four games in 1997, but through the 2008 season, the Angels held a 38–30 advantage in interleague play.

For years, the Dodgers had the tradition and the championship banners to keep the pretenders from Orange County at bay. But after the Halos won the 2002 World Series—with former Dodgers Mike Scioscia and Mickey Hatcher on the coaching staff—all bets were off. When the Angels readopted the original hometown label and started calling themselves the Los Angeles Angels of Anaheim, Dodger fans were indignant.

The Oakland A's received second-class status when they arrived in the Bay Area in 1968, but they quickly established their first-class credentials. For much of the 1970s and 1980s, the A's were the Dodgers' main rival in bringing championships to California. After winning back-to-back titles in 1972 and 1973, Oakland returned to the Fall Classic in 1974 to face the Dodgers. Despite Oakland's championship hardware, the Dodgers believed they were superior—their shrine of a stadium, celebrity fans, and great weather, not to mention 102 wins that season, compared favorably to the A's blue-collar supporters watching players with garish-colored uniforms, long hair, and moustaches in a dingy stadium. But the A's destroyed the Dodgers in five games.

Fourteen years later, the powerful Oakland team of Mark McGwire and Jose Canseco marched into Dodger Stadium against a supposedly outmanned Dodger team. This time Kirk Gibson's miraculous Game One homer and the pitching heroics of Orel Hershiser brought about a historic upset.

Ron Cey attempts to tag Oakland's Sal Bando, 1974 World Series

Oakland's Jose Canseco and Los Angeles' Orel Hershiser, 1988 World Series

Charles Ebbets (left) with co-owner Ed McKeever and Mrs. McKeever, Ebbets Field, April 1913

OWNERS AND GENERAL MANAGERS

Visionaries

Charles Hercules Ebbets rose through the ranks of the Brooklyn organization by the sweat of his brow, going from ticket-taker to magnate in less than two decades. He was rewarded for his work as club secretary with shares of team stock. In 1898, he was made team president (and also served as manager), and he moved the franchise to south Brooklyn to play in a new home: Washington Park.

Ebbets borrowed heavily from investors to keep the team afloat, and by 1907, he had a controlling interest in the team. Six years later, Ebbets solidified his hold on the club legacy when he built a ballpark bearing his name. Ebbets remained owner until his death in 1925.

The team's next great visionary was Larry MacPhail, who was hired as president and general manager in 1938. While with the Cincinnati Reds, MacPhail introduced night baseball to the big leagues. He brought that ingenuity with him to Brooklyn, installing lights at Ebbets Field and putting the Dodgers on the path to success. MacPhail acquired key talents such as Pete Reiser, Joe Medwick, and Dolph Camilli. He also hired radio broadcaster Red Barber from Cincinnati and instituted daily broadcasts of Dodger games. MacPhail, an Ivy Leaguer with a penchant for drink, quarreled frequently with his managers, most notably Leo Durocher. MacPhail left the Dodgers in 1942 to join the army and was replaced by his one-time mentor from their days in the St. Louis Cardinals organization, Branch Rickey.

As brilliant as MacPhail was, his successor may have been the greatest of all baseball visionaries. Known as the Mahatma, Rickey joined the Dodgers as part owner, president, and general manager in 1943 after 17 years as St. Louis' general manager. In addition to spearheading the desegregation of professional baseball, Rickey

Larry MacPhail (left) and Branch Rickey (right)

pioneered the minor league farm system, which he introduced in St. Louis and perfected in Brooklyn. (He is also credited with baseball's later expansion into Latin America.) Rickey was the first general manager to make use of statistics in analyzing player performance. These innovations—the farm system, signing African-American players, and statistical analysis—combined to keep the Dodgers laden with talent for years to come.

Rickey and fellow owner Walter O'Malley were polar opposites who simply despised each other. O'Malley first joined the team as legal counsel in 1942 and bought a piece of the franchise in 1944. A year later, O'Malley, Rickey, and a third partner, John Smith, bought out the Ebbets family estate to give each of them a 25 percent ownership stake. O'Malley and Rickey disagreed on nearly every aspect of the team management—including investing in the Dodgers' spring training facility in Vero Beach, Florida (O'Malley was opposed) and whether to pursue television rights and revenue (Rickey feared it would cut into ballpark attendance). O'Malley gradually squeezed Rickey out, and by 1950, he was the chief stockholder and president. As owner, O'Malley worked hard to promote and market the Dodgers, allowed baseball minds like Buzzie Bavasi to run the team, and in 1957, made one of the most significant moves in sports history when he relocated the Dodgers to California.

General manager Buzzie Bavasi (center) with Don Newcombe and Johnny Podres, November 1955

Walter O'Malley was one of the most influential people in the game throughout the 1960s, but by the end of the decade, the aging owner was grooming his son, Peter, to take his place at the helm of the Dodger organization. The younger O'Malley assumed the president's title in 1970 and became owner upon his father's death in 1979. Peter O'Malley was a new breed of owner. Using marketing techniques honed at Penn's Wharton School of Business, he built the Los Angeles franchise into an archetypical successful baseball operation.

During most of Peter O'Malley's ownership, the team's baseball operations were run by general manager Al Campanis. In his 20 years in the front office (1968–1987), Campanis encouraged a revolutionary approach to player development by emphasizing the fundamentals of the game, such as pitching motion, base running, batting, and defensive techniques. These fundamentals were taught from rookie ball all the way through the major league level, so a player would not be subject to the whims of different managers or coaches in each year of his development. Although this approach helped the team to win four pennants during his tenure as general manager, and although he is credited with discovering

Walter O'Malley (center) with Walter Alston and Pee Wee Reese, 1955 World Series

General manager Al Campanis with Frank Sinatra at Dodger Stadium, October 1977

Peter O'Malley, at the induction of his father into the Baseball Hall of Fame at Cooperstown, July 2008

Sandy Koufax while serving as the Dodgers' scouting director, Campanis is best remembered for the racially insensitive remarks he made during a nationally televised interview in 1987. Two days after stating that African Americans lacked the "necessities" to be baseball managers or executives, Campanis was forced to resign.

In 1998, Rupert Murdoch and his News Corporation purchased the Dodgers for a reported $350 million, the highest amount ever paid for a sports franchise at the time. Murdoch's vision was to run a baseball team like a Hollywood studio, so he brought in Bob Daly from Warner Brothers to serve as the chairman and CEO. News Corp's ownership of the Dodgers was not successful—spending wildly while failing to make the playoffs all six seasons—and in 2004, Boston real estate developer Frank McCourt bought the team for $430 million.

As sole owner, McCourt has invested heavily in renovating Dodger Stadium. He brought in Paul DePodesta, a student of the so-called "Moneyball" approach, to be general manager. DePodesta was very active in the trading and free-agent market—signing J. D. Drew, Jeff Kent, and Derek Lowe—and Los Angeles won the division in 2004, but a disappointing 2005 season led to his dismissal. Since 2006, Ned Colletti has brought in high-profile talent like Andruw Jones, Manny Ramirez, and Takashi Saito, among others, to help the team reclaim its place atop the division.

Frank McCourt shaking hands with manager Joe Torre, opening day, 2008

BREAKING BARRIERS
The Great Experiment and Its Children

The Dodgers would have a revered place in baseball history based solely on their accomplishments. But what separates the franchise from all others is its pioneering role in social progress.

Branch Rickey selected Jackie Robinson as the man with whom he would challenge baseball's longstanding ban on black players, in large measure because of Robinson's college pedigree and national football fame from his days at UCLA. Robinson's strength of character also meant that he would be able to withstand the abuse from those opposed to his presence while resisting the urge to fight back.

Brooklyn was the perfect place for Robinson and the "great experiment." The borough's large black population possessed a certain amount of political and economic clout. And because baseball (and Dodger fandom) was a common experience for the varied ethnic groups that called Brooklyn home, these communities rallied in support of Robinson as an outsider.

Rickey signed Robinson to a contract on October 23, 1945, and after a season with the Montreal Royals in the Dodgers farm system, Robinson made his major league debut on April 15, 1947, playing first base. In the face of near-constant harassment from fans, opposing players, and even teammates, Robinson quickly emerged as a star while helping to revolutionize how the game was played.

Jackie Robinson signing contract, with Branch Rickey

Georgia-born outfielder Dixie Walker was one of the most vocal opponents of Rickey's desegregation efforts, and he tried to rally other Dodger players to resist. But others went out of their way to show their support of Robinson. Second baseman Eddie Stanky, an Alabama native, had the biggest reason to oppose the move, since he and Robinson played the same position, but Stanky fiercely defended his teammate from opponents' barbs. During a game in Philadelphia, he yelled at Phillies manager Ben Chapman to "pick on somebody who can fight back."

Another heroic figure during Robinson's early years was Kentuckian Pee Wee Reese. During a game in Cincinnati early in the 1947 season, when the jeers toward Robinson were particularly vicious, Reese walked over and put his arm around him in a show of solidarity—a legendary gesture in the annals of baseball history.

Spider Jorgensen, Pee Wee Reese, and Eddie Stanky with Jackie Robinson, April 15, 1947

Robinson with the Montreal Royals at spring training, 1946

Jackie Robinson stealing home against the Boston Braves, September 1948

Reggie Smith, 1981

may have caused the team the pennant in 1948. Newcombe was dominating the opposition in the minors, and another top starter could have made the ultimate difference for the big league club in the stretch run against the Boston Braves.

Robinson, Campanella, and Newcombe all started their baseball careers in the Negro Leagues, but soon the Dodgers and other major league teams looked directly to the collegiate and amateur ranks for talent of all races. After their playing days were over, Campanella and Newcombe served prominent roles in the club's front office.

In Los Angeles, the Dodgers' melting-pot environment continued to breed success. With Jim Gilliam at first base, Maury Wills at shortstop, Willie and Tommy Davis in the outfield, and John Roseboro behind the plate, the 1963 championship Dodgers featured five African Americans in the starting lineup—not to mention a Jewish pitcher from Brooklyn as their star on the mound. In the following decades, black stars such as Dusty Baker and Reggie Smith helped to ensure winning ways at Dodger Stadium in the 1970s and 1980s.

In the 1990s, the club broke new ground when it became one of the first teams to tap into the talent base in Asia. In 1995, the Dodgers signed Japanese superstar pitcher Hideo Nomo, who exploded on the scene and thrilled Los Angeles' large Japanese population. The following year he became the first Japanese pitcher to throw a no-hitter in the majors. Nomo's success opened the door for an influx of great Japanese players. Kaz Ishii spent three seasons in Los Angeles and posted a 36–25 record. Takashi Saito became the team's closer in 2006 and was an all-star in 2007, when he notched 39 saves. Hiroki Kuroda of Osaka joined the rotation for an injury-shortened 2008 season.

In 1994, the Dodgers signed Chan Ho Park as the first South Korean to play in the American major leagues. Although Park took exception to some of the rookie hazing he received from Dodger teammates, the burly right-hander has had an effective career. He led the team in wins and strikeouts in 2000 and 2001 before leaving as a free agent in 2002. He returned to Los Angeles in 2008 as a spot starter and reliever.

The first Taiwanese-born player also debuted in a Dodger uniform, and four of Taiwan's five major leaguers have played for Los Angeles. Left fielder Chin-Feng Chen joined the team in 2002 but played in only 19 games through 2005. Pitcher Hong-Chih Kuo was originally signed by the Dodgers in 1999 but didn't make his big league debut until 2005. In 2007, he became the first Taiwanese player to homer in the majors.

Not wanting to push the experiment too far or too fast, Rickey employed a one-black-per-year policy initially. Catcher Roy Campanella and pitcher Don Newcombe both signed contracts with the organization before the 1946 season and were assigned to the farm team in Nashua, New Hampshire. Campanella was called up to join the Dodgers in 1948, and Newcombe followed in 1949. Ironically, Rickey's reluctance to integrate more quickly

Roy Campanella, Cleveland's Larry Doby, Don Newcombe, and Jackie Robinson, 1949 All-Star Game

Hong-Chih Kuo of Taiwan (left) and Takashi Saito of Japan at spring training, 2007

LATIN AMERICAN BALLPLAYERS

The Latin Beat

Baseball's association with Latin America dates back to the turn of the twentieth century. America's expanding influence propped up so-called banana republics and brought baseball to those lands, but it was the Negro Leagues that truly popularized the game south of the border.

Dominican dictator Rafael Trujillo invited a team of barnstorming Negro League stars to play in his country. According to legend, he insinuated that if they lost any games they would be jailed . . . or worse. They went undefeated.

The team's barnstorming tour included trips to Cuba, already a *beisbol* hotbed. One of the first great Cuban players was Havana-born Dolf Luque, who spent two seasons in Brooklyn. He won 14 games in 1930. Al Lopez came out of Florida to play catcher for the Dodgers from 1928 to 1935 and later became a big-league manager.

Branch Rickey was instrumental in expanding the game into Latin America, first by sending his team to play exhibitions in Havana, then by scouting Latin American players. The great Roberto Clemente was originally signed by Brooklyn in 1952 from the Puerto Rican leagues, but the Dodgers failed to see Clemente's potential, and he was claimed by Pittsburgh in the 1954 Rule 5 draft.

Cuban outfielder Sandy Amoros spent seven seasons with the Dodgers and had his most famous moment during the 1955

Al Lopez, circa 1931

Sandy Amoros

World Series, when he robbed Yogi Berra of a hit in Game Seven. Manny Mota, of the Dominican Republic, wore a Dodger uniform from 1969 until 1982, when he retired at the age of 44. He later served as a coach.

Despite these exceptions, the Dodgers were not leaders in recruiting Latino players, even after the club moved to Los Angeles, which had a large Mexican-American population. The Giants were ahead in this regard, but the Dodgers caught up when they established a baseball academy, Campo Las Palmas, in the Dominican Republic during the 1980s. This move helped develop the phenomenal talent that has funneled into the Dodgers' system in recent decades.

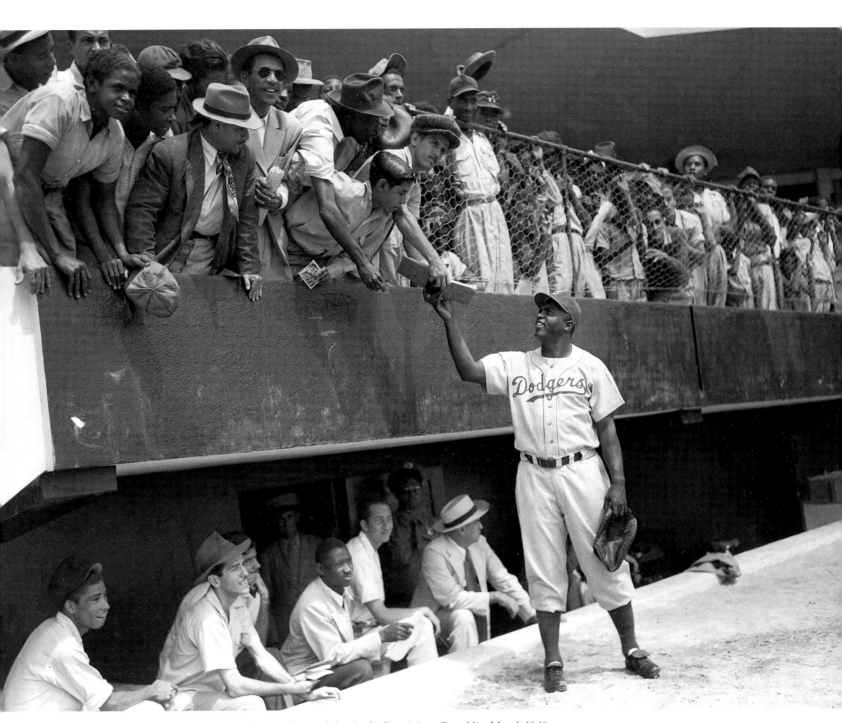

Jackie Robinson signing autographs at spring training in the Dominican Republic, March 1948

Fernando Valenzuela with manager Tommy Lasorda, 1981

Fernando Valenzuela's phenomenal debut in 1981 and continued success throughout the eighties not only helped the Dodgers win on the field, but also made the team more popular with Latinos. The Mexican-born pitcher was the National League Rookie of the Year and Cy Young Award winner in 1981, while pitching Los Angeles to World Series victory. He won 19 games in 1982 and enjoyed his best overall season in 1986 (21–11, 20 complete games, 242 strikeouts).

Valenzuela's legacy was extended in the 1990s with Ramon Martinez of the Dominican Republic and Ismael Valdez of Mexico. Martinez won 20 games in 1990 and seemed headed for Cooperstown, until arm problems shortened his career. In 1993, the Dodgers traded away Ramon's 21-year-old brother Pedro, who went on to become one of the game's top pitchers.

Pedro Guerrero came out of the town of San Pedro de Macoris in the Dominican Republic to become a star outfielder during the 1980s. A three-time 30-home-run hitter, Guerrero was part of a new wave of power hitters from Latin America, which previously produced mostly fast and wiry middle infielders. In June 1985, Guerrero threatened to break Babe Ruth's single-month home run record, and he went on to finish the season with a team-best 33 homers and .320 average.

Dominican-born Raul Mondesi was a five-tool player for the Dodgers in the mid-1990s. He was the 1994 Rookie of the Year when he batted .306 with 27 doubles, and in 1997, he collected 30 homers and 32 stolen bases to become the first Dodger to join the 30–30 club. Two years later he posted career highs with 33 homers, 36 stolen bases, and 99 RBI (and 134 strikeouts).

Third baseman Adrian Beltre, also from the Dominican Republic, was a home run threat in the 2000s and led the National League with 48 dingers in 2004, to go along with a team-high .334 average, 121 RBI, 104 runs, and 200 hits. Venezuelan Cesar Itzuris manned the shortstop position from 2002 to 2005 before Dominican Rafael Furcal took over the job.

Pedro Guerrero, 1985

Raul Mondesi

Rafael Furcal, 2007

Coach Manny Mota, 2006

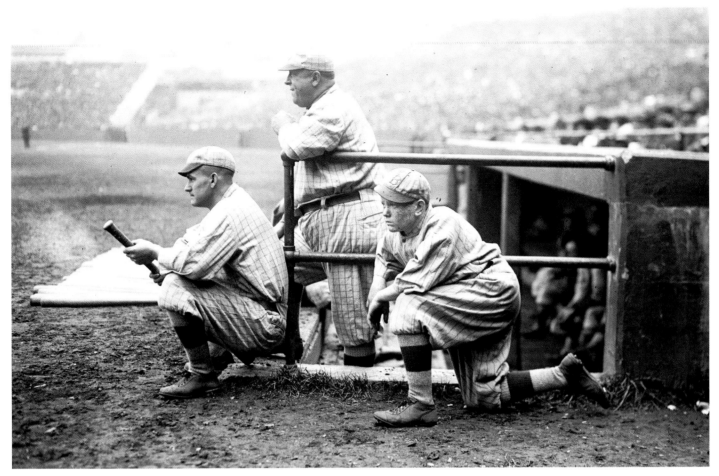

Wilbert Robinson (standing), with Hy Myers and mascot, 1916

DODGER MANAGERS

The Commanders

Brooklyn's first pennants were achieved with little-known Bill McGunnigle at the helm. Under his leadership, the Bridegrooms posted a .658 winning percentage over three seasons, which included an American Association pennant in 1889 and a National League pennant in 1890.

The team's next championship manager was Hall of Famer Ned Hanlon, who suffers from historical disrespect. His 1899 pennant-winning Superbas could go down as one of baseball's great teams, with 101 wins and 47 defeats. But the pre-twentieth-century date inevitably places these accomplishments in the realm of "ancient history." Hanlon led Brooklyn to another pennant in 1900 and followed that with three more winning seasons. By 1904,

the Superbas ceased to be superb, and Hanlon departed after a 104-loss campaign in 1905.

Wilbert Robinson was John McGraw's trusted coach with the Giants, until the two argued at a drunken bash following the team's disappointing loss in the 1913 World Series. Robinson was summarily dismissed, and he headed across town to take the managerial reins in Brooklyn. It was common practice in those days for teams to take on names associated with their leaders or stars, and the Brooklyn club was rechristened the Robins in 1914.

"Uncle Robbie," a comic character in both physical characteristics and demeanor, led his Robins to two National League pennants, though they lost both World Series. He remained

Bill McGunnigle

Leo Durocher (#2) argues a call during the 1941 World Series

the Brooklyn manager through the 1931 season. Robinson passed away in 1934 and was inducted into the Hall of Fame in 1945.

Following brief managerial stints by three former players—including an unsuccessful three-year run by Casey Stengel—Leo Durocher took over as Dodgers manager in 1939. He led the team to the World Series two years later. Throughout the 1940s, "Leo the Lip" argued with umpires while keeping the Dodgers in contention year after year. The amoral Durocher maintained an uneasy alliance with the pious Branch Rickey, but his suspension from the league for gambling in 1947 was too much for "the Mahatma." Durocher returned for the start of the 1948 season but was let go at midseason.

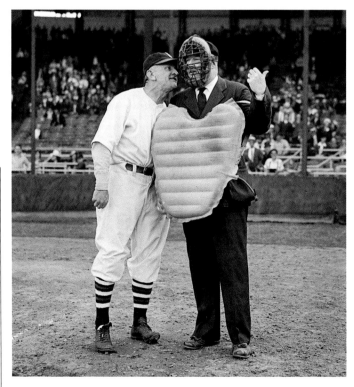

Casey Stengel argues a call, 1938

Chuck Dressen managed the club during the 1951 pennant collapse, but returned the team to the top in 1952 and 1953—only to lose to the Yankees in the World Series both years. Despite winning 298 games in three seasons, Dressen was replaced in 1954 by Walter Alston. Over the next 23 seasons, Alston's Dodgers won seven pennants and four world championships, including the historic 1955 triumph against the Yankees. Even with the success, as one observer noted, "the Dodgers never plan to fire Alston. They prefer to torment him." The club hired Durocher as a coach in 1961, and he and Alston had a volatile relationship over the next four seasons. Alston survived Durocher and his critics, and led the Dodgers to titles in 1963 and 1965. His 2,040 career wins, all with the Dodgers, rank Alston ninth on the all-time list.

Alston's successor, Tommy Lasorda, was more of a Durocher type, with his colorful demeanor and showbiz friendships. But Lasorda got it done on the field too, leading the team to the 1977 and 1978 National League crowns, and World Series wins in 1981 and 1988. Lasorda said he bled Dodger blue, and when he retired after more than two decades on the job, the Dodger magic seemed to go with him. In nearly 20 seasons with Lasorda as manager, the Dodgers won 1,599 games and finished with a losing record only six times.

An inexplicably cheery Chuck Dressen congratulates winning manager Casey Stengel after the 1952 World Series

Former all-star shortstop and Dodger coach Bill Russell stepped in for Lasorda in 1996, but Russell was gone by the All-Star Break in 1998. Dave Johnson was brought in next, and he, too, failed to live up to expectations. The Jim Tracy–Grady Little era from 2001 to 2007 produced winning teams and two postseason appearances, but nothing much beyond that. In 2008, former Yankees manager Joe Torre, a surefire Hall of Famer as a four-time world champion manager, was called upon to resurrect Dodger glory. He got off to a good start, leading the team to a divisional title in his first year on the job.

Walter Alston, circa 1965

Tommy Lasorda argues a call, 1983

Joe Torre, 2008

DODGER CHARACTERS

Bums, Daffiness Boys, and Oddballs

Late in 1912, an outfielder named Charles "Casey" Stengel broke in with the Brooklyn Dodgers. When his team won the pennant in 1916, Stengel apparently lacked faith in their ability to defeat the formidable Boston Red Sox in the World Series. Prior to the series, he asked his teammates what they planned to do with the *loser's* share of the gate receipts. (In 1919, while playing for the Pirates, Stengel acknowledged the razzing of the Ebbets Field crowd at a game by removing his cap, and out flew a sparrow that he had stowed there.)

Stengel wasn't the only character on the 1916 Brooklyn team. Manager Wilbert Robinson was also a bit of a showman, as demonstrated by an incident at spring training that season. A record had been set when a baseball was dropped 504 feet from the top of the Washington Monument, and Charles Ebbets was determined to break that record. For the stunt, he hired aviatrix Ruth Law to fly in her airplane over the field and drop a ball from a distance higher than the previous record. Robinson took on the challenge of catching the orb as it hurtled toward earth.

With a crowd gathered, the plane flew over and the sphere was dropped. It missed Robinson's glove and hit him in the chest with a splatter. Robinson fell to the ground, covered in fluid. "I'm hit!" he exclaimed. His face mask and chest protector were drenched—not with blood and guts, but with grapefruit juice and pulp. Law had forgotten the baseball in her hotel room, and at the last minute she brought a grapefruit instead. (Stengel claimed that the prank was his idea.)

Casey Stengel, circa 1915

Wilbert Robinson, 1916

The Dodgers of the late 1920s and 1930s were commonly known as the "Daffiness Boys" for their goofy characters and often sloppy play. A cornerstone of the "Daffiness Boys" was a pitcher who went by the name of Dazzy. Arthur "Dazzy" Vance was an unusual fellow whose pitching motion resembled a windmill. He also didn't pitch a full big league season until he was 31 years old.

Vance took advantage of the unique visual backdrop at Ebbets Field, which often included laundry hung out to dry. He cut his undersleeves, which he bleached with lye. Between the waving bleached sleeves and flapping linens hanging from clotheslines out of Flatbush apartment houses, "You couldn't hit 'im on a Mundy . . . diapers, undies, sheets flapping on clotheslines—you lost the ball entirely," as Rube Bressler told Lawrence Ritter in *The Glory of Their Times.*

Vance's place as one of the Daffiness Boys was cemented in a 1926 game against Boston. Vance was on second base with Babe Herman at the plate, Hank DeBerry on third, Chick Fewster at first, and nobody out. Herman hit a shot to the right-field wall. DeBerry scored easily. Vance initially held up at second base to make sure the ball wasn't caught. As he finally rounded third base, he realized he was too slow to score, and so he headed back to the bag. Meanwhile, Fewster was motoring into third at the same time. Herman, with his head down, was trying to stretch his hit into a triple. Vance slid back to third, where Fewster was already standing, and then Herman slid in from the other side. The confused third baseman tagged all three men, and a brouhaha ensued. Dazzy looked up from the ground and stated, "Mr. Umpire, fellow teammates, and members of the opposition, if you carefully peruse the rules of our national pastime you will find that there is one and only one protagonist of this hassock; namely yours truly, Arthur C. Vance." He was right. Fewster and Herman were out. Herman had "tripled into a double play."

Dazzy Vance, holding $1,000 in gold for the National League's "golden jubilee," 1926

Lefty O'Doul

Lefty O'Doul, who played for the Dodgers along with many other teams, was a colorful character who helped to forge baseball's popularity in Japan during exhibition tours in the 1930s. After World War II, General Douglas MacArthur said O'Doul's postwar baseball return did more to reconcile the United States and Japan than the efforts of any ambassador.

The Dodgers of the 1950s featured superstars and champions, but one player who might have fit in better with the Daffiness Boys than with the "Boys of Summer" was pitcher Billy Loes. His potential was tremendous, but his performance always below par. Asked why he failed to live up to expectations, Loes said, "Hey, if I win 20, they'll expect me to do it every year."

Pitcher Mike Marshall was a deep thinker who might have been better suited for life in the ivory towers of academia, but he happened to be one of the best relievers in the game. His eccentric views were profiled in Jim Bouton's *Ball Four*. Marshall had a PhD in exercise physiology and was convinced he had developed a new way to pitch that wouldn't stress joints and muscles. Marshall proved his theories on the field, pitching in a record 106 games during his 1974 Cy Young season. Today he runs a special academy for young pitchers designed to develop their pitching motions without injury.

Pennant-winners usually feature great catchers: Yogi Berra, Johnny Bench, Carlton Fisk, and Ivan Rodriguez, among many others. The 1988 world champion Dodgers got by in part with Rick Dempsey behind the plate. Dempsey looked more like a coach or a fan than a hard-nosed catcher. He wore his old-school cap backward but handled pitchers with aplomb. He once got in a fight with Lenny "Nails" Dykstra that resembled the "Thrilla in Manila."

All the talent that Dempsey did not naturally possess was seemingly possessed by Darryl Strawberry. A superstar in New York, he signed with his hometown Dodgers in 1991 and slammed a team-high 28 homers. The next year he was joined by his old pal from high school days, Eric Davis, and Strawberry's career soon resembled a scene from Bret Easton Ellis's novel of drug-addled youth in LA, *Less Than Zero*. The final straw came when Strawberry missed a game to connect with a drug dealer in an Orange County hotel room.

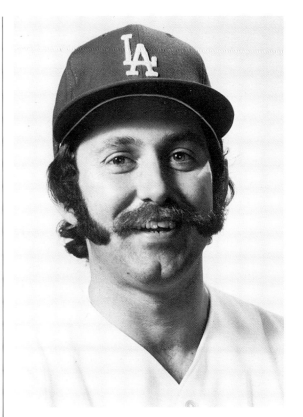

Mike Marshall

Darryl Strawberry with Tommy Lasorda, 1991

NICKNAMES

What's in a Name?

Some people think that all old-time baseball players had nicknames. That's not quite true, although there were plenty of creative ones. The players who were country boys were known as "rubes," so everybody called them Rube. It wasn't a nickname; it was a put-down.

Richard William Marquard was better known as Rube Marquard and was best known for his exploits as a pitcher for the New York Giants, but he came to Brooklyn late in the 1915 season and remained with the club for five more seasons. Rube Bressler, whose parents named him Raymond, batted .302 for the Dodgers from 1928 to 1931.

Throughout the first half of the century, the Brooklyn roster featured plenty of colorful monikers. Charles Stengel was "Casey" because he was from Kansas City (K.C.). Manager Wilbert Robinson was known as "Uncle Robbie." The Robins of the late 1920s and early 1930s offered Babe Herman, Jigger Statz, Sloppy Thurston, Watty Clark, Jumbo Elliott, Lefty O'Doul, Pea Ridge Day, Ownie Carroll, Boom-Boom Beck, Curly Onis, Buzz Boyle, Rabbit

Stanley George "Frenchy" Bordagaray

Richard William "Rube" Marquard

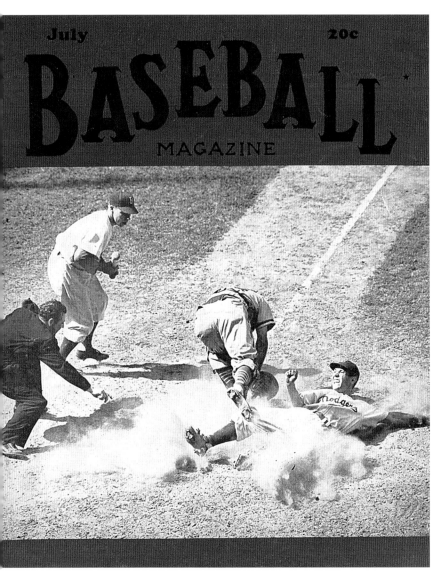

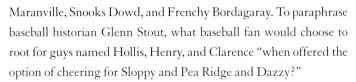

"Pistol Pete" Reiser, 1946

Hideo "The Tornado" Nomo

Maranville, Snooks Dowd, and Frenchy Bordagaray. To paraphrase baseball historian Glenn Stout, what baseball fan would choose to root for guys named Hollis, Henry, and Clarence "when offered the option of cheering for Sloppy and Pea Ridge and Dazzy?"

The great Dodger teams of the 1940s and 1950s featured a "Duke" and a "Preacher" (Snider and Roe), a "Junior" and a "Pee Wee" (Gilliam and Reese), and even a good old-fashioned "Rube" (Walker). Others simply had their last names abbreviated: "Campy" Campanella, "Newk" Newcombe, and the Brooklyn-accented "Oisk" Erskine. Leo "The Lip" Durocher's nickname was derisive and reverent at the same time. "Pistol Pete" Reiser was all speed and hustle. Carl Furillo was bestowed with the names "Skoonj"—evidently in reference to his Italian ancestry and presumed preference for scungilli—and "The Reading Rifle," an homage to his Pennsylvania hometown and his powerful throwing

arm. Later, in Los Angeles, world titles were won by "Dandy Sandy" Koufax and "Big D" Drysdale, with Willie "3-Dog" Davis and "Sweet Lou" Johnson in the outfield.

Most of the really good nicknames dried up by the 1970s. Ron Cey was "The Penguin" and Bill Russell was "Ropes," but you had Steve and Davey on the other side of the infield. Jimmy "The Toy Cannon" Wynn roamed the outfield for two seasons in LA before being sent to Atlanta in exchange for Johnnie B. Baker—you know him as Dusty. Orel Hershiser was a bulldog on the mound in the 1980s, so that's what some people called him: Bulldog.

These days, there are no more "Bambinos" or "Iron Horses," just endless Mikes and Todds and Erics, with a few exceptions. Hideo Nomo's corkscrew delivery earned him the nickname "The Tornado," and Matt Kemp's large size and surprising speed have inspired some to call him "The Bison."

DODGER ROOKIES

A Star Is Born

Zack Wheat, Piedmont Cigarettes baseball card, 1910

Most baseball fans have never heard of Harry Lumley, whose brief and mostly unremarkable career spanned less than six seasons. But as a 23-year-old rookie with the Brooklyn Superbas in 1904, Lumley led the National League with 9 homers and 18 triples. He finished among the top three in home runs in each of the next three seasons and batted .324 in 1906. He was beset by injuries, however, and was out of baseball before he turned 30.

The 22-year-old Zack Wheat (whose younger brother Mack also played in the major leagues) came out of the farm country of Missouri to break into the big leagues in 1909. In 26 games with Brooklyn, the 5-foot-10, 170-pound left-handed-hitting outfielder

Harry Lumley, Ramley Turkish Cigarettes baseball card, 1909

Pete Reiser, circa 1941

swatted .304. By the time he was 25, Wheat was regularly among the top ten hitters in the league.

A couple of Brooklyn stars burst onto the scene with strong rookie campaigns in the late 1920s, but just as quickly faded away. Del Bissonette was a 28-year-old-rookie in 1928 who proceeded to lead the team with 25 homers, 106 runs batted in, and 188 hits. His major league career, during which he posted a .305 lifetime average, was cut short by injuries in 1933. In 1929, a year after Bissonette's debut, rookie Johnny Frederick chipped in 24 homers, 52 doubles, 206 hits, and a .328 average. He continued to produce for Brooklyn but was traded to Sacramento, of the Pacific Coast League, in 1934.

Leo Durocher once said that Pete Reiser was "better than [Willie] Mays." While that observation is hard to justify in light of Mays' legendary career, the fact that such a statement was made by a serious baseball man like Durocher—who managed both men—speaks volumes. Reiser came up through the Dodger system and was slated to be sent to St. Louis. But nobody told manager Durocher, so instead of "hiding" the young outfielder on the bench, Durocher played him. The press was quickly enamored, calling Reiser "Pistol Pete." At that point, there was no way Brooklyn could trade him. After appearing in 58 games as a 21-year-old-rookie in 1940, Reiser exploded in 1941, slamming 39 doubles, 17 triples, and hitting a league-leading .343. He made spectacular catches in the outfield, but he kept colliding with the hard outfield walls. Reiser's injuries kept him from what could have been a Cooperstown-caliber career.

Right: *Jackie Robinson receives the 1947 Rookie of the Year Award from Jack Ryan of the Baseball Writers' Association*

Below: *Ted Sizemore, 1969 Rookie of the Year, on Dodgers program and scorecard, 1970*

In 1947, major league baseball instituted an official Rookie of the Year Award. Over the next 60-plus years, the Dodgers produced 16 winners, including the 1947 winner, Jackie Robinson. The award is now named in Robinson's honor. Three more Dodgers (all African Americans) were named National League Rookie of the Year while the team was in Brooklyn: Don Newcombe (1949), Joe Black (1952), and Junior Gilliam (1953). Black beat out future Hall of Famers Hoyt Wilhelm and Eddie Mathews by posting a 15–4 record and 2.15 ERA.

Frank Howard kicked off his all-star career with 23 homers in 1960 and became the first *Los Angeles* Dodger to bring home the award. Switch-hitting Jim Lefebvre was a career Dodger, and he beat out Joe Morgan for National League Rookie of the Year honors in 1965. Infielder Ted Sizemore was the next Dodger winner, in 1969, although he soon moved on to the Cardinals.

Ten years later, Los Angeles began another dominating run for the award. Four Dodgers were named Rookie of the Year between 1979 and 1982: Rick Sutcliffe, Steve Howe, Fernando Valenzuela, and Steve Sax. Sutcliffe made his career with the Cubs, but Howe, Valenzuela, and Sax were all key contributors to the Dodgers' success over the next several years.

In the 1990s, the Dodgers became the only team ever to produce top rookies five years in a row. Eric Karros' 20 homers and 88 RBI were good enough to win him the award in 1992, and Mike Piazza kicked off a sure Hall of Fame career in 1993 with 35 homers, 112 RBI, and a .318 average. Raul Mondesi continued the trend during the strike-shortened 1994 season, and Hideo Nomo became the first Asian player to win a major award in the United States, thanks to a 13–6 record in 1995. Todd Hollandsworth batted .233 in "the Show" for 41 games in 1995, but his first full season in 1996 produced numbers good enough for a fifth straight Dodger rookie honor.

Right: *Hideo Nomo, with Rachel Robinson, receives the 1995 Rookie of the Year Award*

Steve Howe, 1981

Carl Furillo, with Branch Rickey, signs new contract, February 1950

SALARIES
They Don't Call 'Em Pros for Nothing

In the 1880s, nearly all professional baseball players were covered by the "reserve clause," which meant they were essentially the property of the club they played for, even after their contracts ran out. John Montgomery Ward, who spent most of his career with the Giants, vocally opposed the system and formed baseball's first union, the Brotherhood of Professional Base Ball Players, in 1885. The union did not last, however, and it would be another 81 years before the modern Major League Baseball Player's Association was formed.

Jackie Robinson's monthly salary when he signed with the Dodgers organization in 1946 was $600, and he received a $3,500 signing bonus. In the winter following his first season in the majors, Robinson made $100,000 in endorsements, speaking engagements, and film contracts.

Right fielder Carl Furillo received a reported $20,000 raise after batting .322 with 106 RBI in 1949. Many players came to rely on the World Series shares, which seemed to be almost guaranteed for Dodgers of that era. The share from the attendance-record-breaking 1959 World Series was $11,231 per player.

In 1966, Sandy Koufax and Don Drysdale jointly held out for a combined $1.05-million, three-year deal. During the stalemate with general manager Buzzie Bavasi, the two pitchers were spotted all over town and even made the movie *Warning Shot* with David Janssen. Drysdale threatened to join the Screen Actor's Guild and make movies his full-time occupation, and both pitchers suggested that they didn't need baseball to make a living. Bavasi retorted, "Good luck." Drysdale fielded an offer from Japan but in the end settled for a one-year, $110,000 deal. Koufax got a little more. That season, Drysdale was 13–16; Koufax was 27–9.

Pitcher Andy Messersmith, a graduate of Western High School in Anaheim and the University of California, was a key player in toppling baseball's reserve clause. After the Dodgers refused to include a no-trade clause in his contract during negotiations before the 1975 season, Messersmith sued the Dodgers for the right to sign with another team. An arbitrator ruled in Messersmith's favor, and the era of free agency was born.

Fernando Valenzuela was one of baseball's premier pitchers in the mid-1980s, and his peak salary was just over $2 million in 1988. A year later, Orel Hershiser became the highest paid player in baseball with an annual salary of nearly $2.8 million.

In December 1998, general manager Kevin Malone signed Kevin Brown to an outrageous $105-million contract, and threw in an airplane for his family. The pitcher's $10.7 million salary in the first year and $15.7 million per year thereafter made him the highest paid National Leaguer for four years running. Shawn Green was not far behind, earning just shy of $10 million in 2000; by 2004, Green was hauling in $16.7 million, third most in the league. Mike Piazza, who earned $126,000 as a rookie in 1993, made $8 million per season by his last year in LA.

Pitcher Jason Schmidt signed a free-agent contract worth in excess of $15.7 million prior to the 2007 season. He won one game for the Dodgers in an injury-shortened campaign, earning him $611,048 per inning pitched. Rafael Furcal's $13.7 million paycheck in 2008 was second only to Schmidt's, and Furcal sat out all but 32 games with injuries.

Kevin Brown, 1998

Don Drysdale (left) and Sandy Koufax (right) meet with director Buzz Kulik of Paramount Studios in Hollywood, March 1966

HIT MEN

Hitting Them Where They Ain't

Wee Willie Keeler

Zack Wheat batted above .300 six times in his first ten full seasons in Brooklyn, with a high of .335 in 1918. Between 1920 and 1925 he never hit below .320 and posted .375 marks in an injury-shortened 1923 and again in 1924. Not counting the aborted 1923 season, Wheat averaged 201 hits from 1920 to 1925. He is the all-time franchise record holder in hits, doubles, triples, and total bases, and Wheat ranks among the leaders in most other hitting categories.

Pitchers saw little humor in having to face original "Daffiness Boy" Babe Herman during the late 1920s. The 180-pound right-hander cranked out 217 hits, 42 doubles, and a .381 average in

Zack Wheat

Baseball prior to 1920 is known as the "dead-ball" era, but Wee Willie Keeler made the most of it by hitting the ball "where they ain't." Joining the Brooklyn club in 1899, Keeler went on to have three straight seasons with more than 200 base hits while batting .360 during that span.

Looking at baseball's offensive statistics during the 1920s and 1930s, one might suspect that sometime in the early 1920s, performance-enhancing drugs started making the rounds in clubhouses throughout the league. What actually happened: In response to the 1919 "Black Sox" scandal and Babe Ruth's popularizing the long ball, "outlaw" pitches like spitballs were, well, outlawed, and the ball itself was livened up with tighter twine and a "rabbit" cork in the middle.

Steve Garvey

Tommy Davis

1929. He improved on that in the hitter-friendly season of 1930, when he produced 241 hits, 35 homers, 130 RBI, 143 runs scored, and a .393 average—all career highs.

Tommy Davis could hit in all directions. With his downward cut, he was a line-drive phenom, and the dimensions of the field mattered little. In 1962, the Brooklyn-born Davis put together one of the greatest all-around offensive seasons: .346 average, 230 hits, 27 homers, 120 runs scored, and 153 RBI. Somehow, he finished third in the MVP voting behind teammate Maury Wills and Willie Mays. In 1965, Davis suffered a serious leg injury that sidelined him for the season and may have cost him a plaque in Cooperstown.

First baseman Steve Garvey batted above .300 and collected at least 200 hits in all but one season from 1974 to 1980. The 10-time all-star never won a batting title or home run crown in his career.

Since Garvey left, only one Dodger has had a 200-hit season: Mike Piazza, with 201 in 1997. Piazza spent five full seasons in Los Angeles and led the squad in both average and homers in each one. His .362 average in 1997 was the highest mark by a Dodger in more than 60 years.

THE HOME RUN
"He Got All of It"

Viewed in the context of the performance-enhanced 1990s and 2000s, the long-ball numbers of Dodgers past seem almost quaint—all-time franchise leader Duke Snider never hit more than 43 homers in a season. Go back to the pre-1920s era, and it's almost as if they were playing a different sport.

The Brooklyn ballclubs of the American Association never had much in the way of home run hitters, even by dead-ball standards. During the team's first season in the National League in 1890, Thomas "Oyster" Burns exploded with 13 homers—more than anyone else in the league that year, and the most of Burns' career. Burns was Brooklyn's last home run champ until the opening decade of the next century, when Jimmy Sheckard, Harry Lumley, and Tim Jordan all took a turn as National League homer king.

Zack Wheat was the team leader in dingers eight times and was the franchise's career home run king for decades, but his

Gil Hodges, 1951

single-season high mark was 16 homers in 1922. The following season, as the lively ball took hold, Jack Fournier became the first Dodger to top 20 homers in a season, a feat he duplicated in each of the next two seasons, including a then-franchise-record high of 27 in 1924.

A man named Babe became the main power threat for Brooklyn after Fournier. Although a far cry from his namesake in the Bronx, Babe Herman slammed 35 homers for the Dodgers in 1930, and he finished among the top ten in the National League in all but one of his six seasons in Brooklyn.

The Dodger teams of the 1950s boasted tremendous home run power. Although they had only one home run king during

Manager Wilbert Robinson with Jack Fournier and Zack Wheat, 1921

the decade—Duke Snider in 1956—as a team, the Dodgers led all others in every season from 1949 to 1955. Snider slammed 40 or more homers in five consecutive seasons (1953–1957) while also finishing among the NL's top five in slugging percentage each year. When the Dodgers moved to Snider's hometown of LA, however, the dimensions of their new ballpark, the Coliseum, destroyed him.

Snider's main brothers-in-arms during the fifties were Gil Hodges and Roy Campanella. Both Snider and Hodges ranked among the league's top ten in homers for nine straight seasons (1949–1957), and Hodges twice hit 40 or more in a season. In his MVP season of 1953, Campanella hit a career-high 41, but trailed both Snider and Eddie Mathews for the league lead.

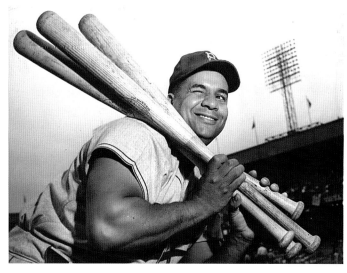

Roy Campanella

Duke Snider at bat, 1952 World Series

Frank Howard at bat, 1963 World Series

Hodges' and Snider's home-run production dipped dramatically after the team moved to Los Angeles in 1958, and the team's home run totals took a further hit with the move to the spacious confines of Dodger Stadium in 1962. Frank Howard seemed to adjust to the new surroundings and clubbed a team-high 31 home runs that year. He was the first West Coast Dodger to break the 30-homer plateau and the last to do so for more than a decade

The Dodgers of the 1960s won mostly with pitching and speed, but by 1974, they were blasting more long balls than any other National League squad, led by Jimmy Wynn's 32. The pinnacle of Dodger power during the decade came in 1977, when Steve Garvey (33), Reggie Smith (32), Ron Cey (30), and Dusty Baker (30) became the first foursome from one team to hit 30 or more homers in the same season. The switch-hitting Smith—like Snider, a native of Compton—led the way in 1978 with 29 homers. None of the four had another 30-homer season in their careers, although as a team the Dodgers continued to out-homer all other National League squads.

Mike Piazza

Shawn Green, 2001

Four Dodger home runs in Game Two of the 1977 World Series (clockwise from upper left): Ron Cey, Steve Yeager, Steve Garvey, and Reggie Smith

The depth of the Dodger power surge never matched the teams of the 1950s and 1970s, but there have been plenty of sluggers sporting Dodger blue. Pedro Guerrero blasted more than 30 homers three times in four years (1982, '83, and '85), and UCLA's Eric Karros ranks third on the all-time franchise list with 270 homers as a Dodger—although some critics contend that his long balls too often came when a game was already decided. In 1992, Karros accounted for more than one-fourth of the team's homer total.

Raul Mondesi was another consistent slugger for Los Angeles, belting as many as 33 homers in 2000, but he never finished among the league's top ten—a sign of the era's statistical inflation. The 1997 lineup had four guys with 30 or more homers, paced by

Mike Piazza's 40. Todd Zeile, a native of the valley and a UCLA product, chipped in with 31 during his lone full season with the Dodgers. Four years earlier, Piazza set the franchise record for homers by a rookie, with 35.

Gary Sheffield averaged 37 homers a year for the Dodgers during the height of the steroid era (1998–2001). Shawn Green, a local kid from Orange County, did not have the body of a steroid abuser, and no Dodger has ever hit more homers in one season (49) than Green did in 2001; he also hit four in one game that year. Adrian Beltre set the Dodger record for four-baggers by a righty, knocking 48 dingers during his free-agent year of 2005. He never hit more than 26 in any other season.

DODGER DEFENSE

With These Hands

It is often said that defense and pitching win championships, and while defense is a skill that can be difficult to judge with statistics, the pennant-winning Brooklyn teams of 1889 and 1890 had fewer errors than any other team in the league. A later Brooklyn pennant winner, the 1916 team, was led by a slick-fielding first baseman named Jake Daubert.

The Dodgers of "Daffiness Boys" fame were not known as defensive geniuses; rather, much of their comical image was built on miscues committed in the field. When Leo Durocher arrived as manager, that all came to an end. Durocher, who in his playing days was a light-hitting shortstop who survived by virtue of his fielding prowess, emphasized solid defense. This was embodied by the great young shortstop, Pee Wee Reese, and third baseman Billy Cox.

The "Boys of Summer" certainly did their share of mashing, but airtight fielding was their secret to success. In addition to Reese, Gil Hodges and Jackie Robinson were the cornerstones of an infield that helped Brooklyn lead the league in fielding five times between 1949 and 1956. The Gold Glove Award was instituted in 1957, and Hodges took the honor for first basemen in the first three years of the award. Catcher Roy Campanella had a gun for an arm, and right fielder Carl Furillo was known as "The Reading Rifleman" for his own high-caliber arm (and his Reading, Pennsylvania, origins). In center field, Duke Snider mastered Ebbets Field's odd outfield configuration for a decade.

Wes Parker grew up in posh Brentwood and, with his movie-star good looks, was a ladies' man who might have made

Steve Garvey stretches to make the out, 1978 World Series

Raul Mondesi, 1995

Gil Hodges, Pee Wee Reese, and Roy Campanella practice fielding, with Carl Furillo, at spring training

it in the movies. But instead of going to Hollywood, he begged his neighbor, a Kansas City Royals scout, to sign him to a baseball contract. Parker's glove work attracted attention in the minors, and he was signed by the Dodgers in 1963. In his rookie season, Parker ousted Ron Fairly from the first base position and went on to win the Gold Glove Award every year from 1967 to 1972.

Don Drysdale was a great all-around athlete who could hit and field as well as pitch. His pickoff move was unparalleled. In his heyday, Andy Messersmith was the hardest throwing right-handed pitcher in the league, and his fielding prowess on the mound was legendary.

Steve Garvey was a disaster at third base, so the team tried him out at first base. He beat out Bill Buckner on the strength of hard work and developed into a fine first-sacker. Garvey won four straight Gold Gloves from 1974 to 1977. During the 1990s, outfielder Raul Mondesi had one of the best arms in baseball, and he put fear in the hearts of many an opposing base runner.

CATCHERS
Behind the Dish

L owell Otto "Moonie" Miller spent his entire career with Brooklyn (1910–1922) and nearly every game as a catcher. Unfortunately for Miller, all that most baseball historians know about him is that he was the player that Bill Wambsganss tagged for the third out in the unassisted triple-play during the 1920 World Series. Another longtime Dodger catcher that is best remembered for a blunder is Mickey Owen. Although he was a four-time all-star with Brooklyn, Owen's passed ball during the 1941 World Series was the pivotal moment in the Dodgers' loss to the Yankees.

Al Lopez, 1939

Otto Miller, 1920

Al Lopez first joined the Dodgers as a nineteen-year-old in 1928, and he assumed the starting catcher's job in 1930, a position he held for six seasons. Lopez twice batted over .300 and made the all-star team in 1934 before going on to a long career with the Braves and Pirates.

Roy Campanella is one of baseball's all-time greats. The New Jersey native was a star for the Baltimore Elite Giants of the Negro Leagues before being signed by Branch Rickey in 1946. He made his major-league debut in 1948. Campanella's half-black, half-Italian background helped make him a fan favorite in Brooklyn—but what really made him popular was his booming bat and stellar defense. Three times, Campy was named the National League's Most Valuable Player (1951, 1953, 1955), and although he led the league in a major offensive category only once in his career (142 RBI in 1953), Campanella made the all-star team every season from 1949 to 1956. The future Hall of Famer's career came to an abrupt end when he was paralyzed in a car accident in January 1958, at the age of 35. The wheelchair-bound Campanella was honored in front of a record crowd at LA Memorial Coliseum in May 1959, an event that is still considered one of the most memorable moments in Los Angeles sports history. After his playing days were over, Campanella continued to work for the club. His lifelong connection with the Dodgers exemplifies the familial nature of the franchise.

Right: *Roy Campanella makes the tag*

Mickey Owen makes a putout during the 1941 World Series

John Roseboro blocks the plate against Frank Robinson, June 1958

Steve Yeager blocks the plate against Paul Blair, 1978 World Series

John Roseboro learned from and idolized Campy, and he handled well the pressure of replacing the Dodger icon. Roseboro was a decent hitter, but his fielding ability and excellent handling of the pitching staff are what set him apart. The soft-spoken Roseboro understood the game and communicated with his pitchers through body language and looks. Sandy Koufax and Don Drysdale swore by him.

Joe Ferguson, who grew up in the Bay Area rooting for the hated Giants, was drafted by the Dodgers in 1968 and became the team's regular catcher in 1973. He shared catching duties with Steve Yeager, but Yeager, the superior defensive player, eventually won the job, and Ferguson was moved to the outfield. Ferguson's greatest moment came while playing right field. In Game One of the 1974 World Series against Oakland, a fly ball was hit toward center fielder Jim Wynn, whose arm was hanging. Knowing Wynn had no shot at making the throw, Ferguson cut in front of him, made the catch, and unloaded one of the best throws in World Series history—to Yeager, who was blocking the plate masterfully—to nail Sal Bando at home.

Yeager was not a great threat with the bat (evidenced by his .228 career average), but in the 1970s, he was second to only Johnny Bench when it came to defensive catchers in the National League. Yeager's tinted glasses, curly hair, and irreverent attitude made him the perfect "Hollywood Dodger." Tragedy was narrowly avoided when a jagged slice of broken bat lodged in Yeager's throat while he waited in the on-deck circle during a game at Wrigley Field in 1976. He recovered, and when he returned to play, he added a hanging shield below his catcher's mask to protect his throat. This shield continues to be a standard piece of catcher's equipment today.

With the aging Yeager increasingly hampered by injuries, Mike Scioscia stepped in to take the starting role. A former high school football star recruited by Joe Paterno at Penn State, the tough Scioscia was a Tommy Lasorda favorite. He broke into the big leagues in 1980 and was the main starter during the 1981 championship season. His best batting average was .296 in 1985, but his most important jobs were to play defense and handle the Los Angeles pitching staff. Scioscia spent his entire playing career with the Dodgers and is the franchise leader in games played at the catcher's position.

Mike Scioscia, July 1992

Mike Piazza blocks the plate against Sammy Sosa, April 1996

Mike Piazza could always hit, but when he was drafted by Lasorda—in the sixty-second round in 1988—as a favor to his friend, Piazza's dad, the manager had to convince the club, and Mike himself, that Piazza could be made into a major league catcher. Piazza worked day and night, and while nobody will confuse him with Yeager or Bench, he was a credible big-league backstop for more than a decade. What cannot be doubted is that he was one of the best hitting catchers in the history of the game. Piazza won the Rookie of the Year Award in 1993 by hitting 35 homers and driving in 112 runs. His .318 batting average that year was his lowest mark in five seasons with Los Angeles; his peak season was 1997, when he batted .362 while notching a career-best 40 homers. An all-star and Silver Slugger Award winner in every season as a Dodger, Piazza was traded to Florida during the 1998 season because the team was worried that it would not be able to sign him as a free agent after the season.

Paul Lo Duca emerged as the regular starter behind the plate in 2001 and spent three-and-a-half seasons with Los Angeles before being traded to Florida in 2004. His best season was his first one with LA, when he belted 25 homers, drove in 90 runs, and hit .320—all career highs.

Russell Martin is the latest in a long line of great Dodger catchers. In 2007, the Canadian-born backstop won the Gold Glove and Silver Slugger Awards in just his second season and was the team leader in RBI. He earned a second straight all-star selection in 2008 and led the team in on-base percentage.

Paul Lo Duca tags out Colorado's Terry Shumpert, August 2001

Russell Martin, July 2008

First Basemen

First Sackers

The name Candy LaChance sounds more likely to be found on the marquee of a burlesque show than on a baseball card, but George "Candy" LaChance manned the first base position for Brooklyn during the 1890s. He batted over .300 three times between 1894 and 1897 and exhibited some home-run power, by dead-ball standards.

From 1910 until 1918, Jake Daubert was a steady hand at first base and a force at the plate. Although he twice led the National League in batting and hit above .300 seven times with Brooklyn, his accomplishments are overlooked in an era that featured the likes of Ty Cobb, Joe Jackson, and Tris Speaker. Daubert's .350

average and .405 on-base percentage in 1913 helped earn him the Most Valuable Player Award.

Brooklyn acquired first baseman Jack Fournier from the Cardinals in 1923. Although weak with the glove, Fournier was the Robins' top home run hitter and RBI threat every season from 1923 to 1925, including a league-best 27 homers in 1924. He also batted .345 over that span.

San Francisco–native Dolph Camilli was coming off a season in which he batted .339 with 27 homers when the Dodgers acquired him from Philadelphia in March 1938. He proceeded to drive in more than 100 runs in four of the next five seasons while

Jake Daubert, 1914

averaging nearly 27 home runs per year. His peak came in 1941, when he led the National League with 34 homers and 120 RBI and brought home league MVP honors. (Camilli's son, Gino, was the first Dodger to step to bat when the club played its first West Coast game against San Francisco at Seals Stadium in 1958.)

Gil Hodges is a true Brooklyn and New York icon. His first, brief turn with the Dodgers was as a 19-year-old third baseman in 1943, and after serving in World War II, Hodges returned to Brooklyn as a catcher in 1947. He made the move to first base in 1948 (thanks in part to the arrival of Roy Campanella) and then hit his stride in 1949, knocking 23 homers and driving in 115 runs. Hodges went on to collect at least 100 RBI in each of the next six seasons and hit more than 30 homers six times in seven years. In 1954, he notched career-high marks in homers (42), RBI (130), and batting average (.304). Despite being one of the elite power hitters of his era, an eight-time all-star, and a three-time Gold Glove Award winner, Hodges has not been honored with induction into baseball's Hall of Fame in Cooperstown.

After spending most of his first four seasons playing outfield for the Dodgers, Ron Fairly stepped in to fill Hodges' shoes at first base in 1962, until the slick-fielding Wes Parker came on the scene in 1965 and pushed Fairly back to the outfield. Parker's eight seasons at first base were followed by another converted outfielder, Bill Buckner, but Buckner's role as Dodger first-sacker was short-lived due to the emergence of Steve Garvey.

Dolph Camilli, 1938

Gil Hodges, 1952

Wes Parker, 1971

Steve Garvey

As a kid in Tampa, Florida, Garvey rode the Dodgers' spring training bus, which was driven by his father. The young Garvey grew up idolizing Gil Hodges, and Garvey's manner reminded many of the elder first baseman.

After batting .304 in 114 games in 1973, Garvey emerged as a star in 1974. He was a write-in selection to start in the All-Star Game and won the game's MVP award. He finished the season with a .312 average, 200 hits, and 111 RBI while leading Los Angeles to the World Series. Garvey was named the 1974 National League Most Valuable Player and won his first of four straight Gold Gloves. When Tommy Lasorda took over as manager in 1976, he asked Garvey to hit for greater power. Garvey responded with 33 homers in 1977, although his average dropped below .300—to .297. His home run total fell to 21 in 1978, and his batting average spiked back to .315; he also posted a career-best .499 slugging percentage.

Franklin Stubbs

Eric Karros, 1998

James Loney, 2008

Garvey's successor, Greg Brock, had decent power—he belted 21 homers in 438 at bats in 1985—but his batting average never topped .251 in four seasons with LA. After Brock was traded to Milwaukee in 1986, the first-base job went to Franklin Stubbs, a collegiate superstar whose professional career never quite lived up to the hype. Stubbs was another high-power, low-average hitter and failed to get a firm hold on the position.

Stubbs was replaced by a Hall of Famer. Although he was nearing the end of his career by the time he arrived in LA, Eddie Murray posted a solid all-star season in 1990, batting a career-best .300 to go along with 26 home runs and 95 RBI.

The 1992 NL Rookie of the Year, Eric Karros played more games at first base for the Dodgers than anybody except Gil Hodges. He was a consistent power threat throughout the 1990s and had five seasons with at least 30 homers and 100 RBI. He was also steady with the glove.

The revolving door of first basemen that followed Karros' 11-year stint included former all-star Fred McGriff, former all-star and converted outfielder Shawn Green, and former all-star and converted shortstop Nomar Garciaparra. Garciaparra had 20 homers and a .303 average in his first season as a first baseman, in 2006. The 33-year-old Garciaparra shifted to third base in 2007 to make room for 23-year-old James Loney at first base. Loney's .331 average and 15 home runs in 96 games put him in contention for Rookie of the Year honors in 2007—although his 13 errors in 2008 were more than Steve Garvey ever had in his 14 seasons at first base.

Bill Dahlen, 1910

SECOND BASEMEN AND SHORTSTOPS
Up the Middle

Solid up-the-middle play has always been the Dodger Way—and it was also the Superbas' way during their 1899 and 1900 pennant seasons. Second baseman Tom Daly began his career as a catcher, but ended up playing nearly 800 games at the keystone position for Brooklyn. Shortstop Bill Dahlen had his best seasons while with the Cubs, but his speed on the bases and solid glove work in the field made him an essential contributor to Brooklyn's success as well. He later managed the team from 1910 to 1913.

Billy Herman is probably the best second basemen you've never heard of. A superstar with the Cubs, Herman was traded to the Dodgers for a song in 1941 and helped steer the team to the pennant that year. In 1943, he hit .330 and drove in a career-best 100 runs. After serving in the U.S. Navy in 1944 and 1945,

he returned briefly to the Dodgers in 1946 before being traded to the Braves.

Eddie Stanky, another former Cub, filled in for Herman during the war years and then held the Dodgers' second-base position through 1947. The 5-foot-8 Stanky drew a ton of walks, including a franchise record 148 in 1945; that same year, he also led the league with 128 runs scored. Stanky was nicknamed "the Brat," and Leo Durocher called him "my kind of player." Stanky was eventually traded to the Braves in 1948 to clear the way for Jackie Robinson.

Pee Wee Reese manned the shortstop position alongside Herman, Stanky, Robinson, and others. He was selected to the all-star team in 1942, then left to join the Navy after the season. When he returned after three years in the service, Reese picked up where

Billy Herman, 1941

Pee Wee Reese and Junior Gilliam

he left off and was named an all-star every season from 1946 to 1953. He spent his entire career with the Dodgers and ranks as the franchise's all-time leader in runs scored and walks, is second in hits and at bats, and third in games played.

Jackie Robinson's contribution to professional baseball cannot be overstated. More than just the first African American to play in the major leagues, his play on the field was pure greatness. As a 28-year-old rookie in 1947, he batted .297 with 125 runs scored and a league-high 29 stolen bases, and he earned the Rookie of the Year trophy. Two years later, he was named Most Valuable Player by finishing among the league leaders in most major categories, including the only batting crown of his Hall of Fame career. Robinson ran the bases with speed, guile, and aggression. His versatility is exemplified by the fact that he was the Dodgers' regular starter at four different positions during his career, depending on what the team needed. He came up as a first baseman in 1947 but moved to second base to make room for Gil Hodges. When Jim "Junior" Gilliam was called up in 1953, Robinson moved to the outfield, until Sandy Amoros' arrival meant that Jackie's services were most needed at the hot corner.

Jackie Robinson

Junior Gilliam, 1956 World Series

Robinson's replacement at second base, Gilliam, spanned the Brooklyn and Los Angeles eras. He was the only position player in the starting lineup for all four Dodger championship teams of the 1950s and 1960s, and he, like Robinson, succeeded wherever he was needed in the field: second base during the 1955 and 1963 seasons, third base in 1959 and 1965. (He also had a stint in left field in 1958.) Gilliam batted .300 only once, but his keen eye and base-running ability meant he was always a threat to take a base any way he could, whether on four balls or with stolen bases.

When it comes to speed on the bases, few did it better than Gilliam's infield compatriot, Maury Wills. Shortstop Wills stole

104 bases in 1962—breaking Ty Cobb's single-season record—en route to the MVP award. It was Wills' third of six consecutive years leading the league in thefts. He also notched career highs in runs (130), hits (208), triples (10), home runs (6), and runs batted in (48) in 1962, while winning his second straight Gold Glove Award.

The combination of Davey Lopes and Bill Russell was key to the Dodgers' success in the 1970s. The two played side by side from 1973 through 1981, including four World Series teams. Russell was originally an outfielder, but manager Walt Alston took a chance that Russell was the man to replace Wills at short. He went on to play nearly 1,750 games at the position; his 2,181 total games for

Maury Wills (#30) stealing second base

Bill Russell and Davey Lopes, 1978 World Series

the franchise are second only to Zack Wheat. Lopes, who played more games at second base than any Dodger in history, was a four-time all-star with a combination of speed and power. Although his stolen bases don't quite stack up, Lopes had speed that some say was greater than Wills'.

Lopes was traded to Oakland before the 1982 season to make way for Steve Sax, who went on to become the 1982 Rookie of the Year and a Los Angeles fan favorite. Sax had an all-star career with the Dodgers until a strange affliction caused him to make wild throws to first base on routine plays.

With the exception of Sax, the Dodger middle infield had little consistency following the Lopes-Russell era. In the late 1980s and early 1990s, Alfredo Griffin fit the mold of the slick-fielding Latino shortstop. Griffin was succeeded by fellow countryman Jose Offerman. Both Griffin and Offerman stole a lot of bases, but they also got caught often. In 2004, Venezuelan Cesar Izturis became the first Dodger infielder since Lopes to win a Gold Glove Award. Other than an injury-shortened 2008, Dominican Rafael Furcal has effectively manned the shortstop spot for Los Angeles since 2006.

Second baseman Jeff Kent, a local boy from Edison High in Huntington Beach, signed with his hometown Dodgers as a free agent before the 2005 season. The powerful line-drive hitter is a contender for the Hall of Fame, largely for his power and RBI numbers.

Rafael Furcal (#15) and Jeff Kent turn two, September 2006

THIRD BASEMEN
The Hot Corner

Third base has all too often been a problem position for the Dodgers. George Pinckney handled the chores for the Brooklyn club from 1886 to 1891. He hit 7 homers and 83 RBI (high marks in that era) for the 1890 National League champs, and his 280 career stolen bases rank sixth on the all-time franchise list.

Cookie Lavagetto's career-defining moment came in Game Four of the 1947 World Series when he knocked the game-

Billy Cox, 1953 World Series

Ron Cey, 1981 World Series

winning hit against the Yankees, but he also was a four-time all-star at third base.

Without question, the two best third basemen in Dodger history are Billy Cox and Ron Cey. Cox was a glove man extraordinaire from 1948 to 1954. A .262 career hitter, he batted .302 in 15 World Series games for Brooklyn.

Other than Jim Gilliam, who played more than 750 games at the hot corner, third base resembled a revolving door until the arrival of Ron Cey. The 5-foot-10, 185-pounder had a funny walk that led people to call him "Penguin." Cey broke into the majors in 1971 but found himself in a battle for the third base job with Steve Garvey. The team quickly realized that both men needed to play—and also that Garvey couldn't make the throw from third base—so Garvey was sent across the diamond to man first base.

Adrian Beltre, July 1999

Cey hit 20 or more homers in every season from 1975 to 1985 (other than the strike-shortened 1981 campaign), and he ranks fifth on the career franchise list with 228 home runs. Cey was steady with the glove and clutch with the bat. He batted .350 in the 1981 World Series to earn a share of series MVP honors.

Adrian Beltre was a fine hitter in his first five seasons as the Dodger third baseman. In 2004, his final year under contract with the team, he exploded with career highs of 200 hits, 48 homers, 121 RBI, 104 runs, a .334 average, and a .629 slugging percentage; he finished second to Barry Bonds in the MVP voting. (A year later, Beltre signed a contract with the Seattle Mariners worth nearly $13 million per year.) In 2008, Blake DeWitt became the latest to take over the position. The 22-year-old rookie contributed in 95 games at third for the division champs.

Blake DeWitt, April 2008

Duke Snider (left) makes a leaping catch against the wall as Carl Furillo watches at Ebbets Field, 1955

OUTFIELDERS
Roaming the Outer Pastures

In the 125 years of Dodger history, the outfield position has featured its share of all-stars, from power-hitting sluggers to scrappy speedsters. Brooklyn's championship squads of 1889 and 1890 lacked any Hall of Famers in the outfield, but right fielder Oyster Burns was a lifetime .300 hitter whose 13 homers and 128 RBI were tops in the league in 1890. Mike Griffin joined Burns in 1891 and played for Brooklyn through 1898. He led the way with a .358 average in 1894.

After Brooklyn acquired several players from the Baltimore Orioles in the late 1890s (when the teams shared an owner), the outfield boasted two future Hall of Famers. Willie Keeler was a premier hitter of his era, perhaps best remembered for his saying, "hit 'em where they ain't." The lesser known of the Hall of Fame transplants from Baltimore, Joe Kelley, hit .317 during his career and possessed both speed and power.

Zack Wheat played more games in a Dodgers (or Robins or Superbas) uniform than anybody else in history and reached base more times than any other. During his 18 seasons with Brooklyn, Wheat was teamed with numerous outfield compatriots, including

Casey Stengel and Hy Myers. While Stengel is best known for his later exploits as a manager, Myers is largely forgotten. But Myers spent nearly a decade with the Dodgers and led the majors in slugging (.436), triples (14), and RBI (73) in 1919.

Brooklyn outfielders Casey Stengel, Jimmy Johnston, Hy Myers, Zack Wheat, 1916

Leo Durocher's 1941 pennant winners featured an elite outfield of Joe "Ducky" Medwick, Fred "Dixie" Walker, and "Pistol" Pete Reiser. (Reiser's achievements are discussed in the section on "Dodger Rookies.") Medwick earned his Hall of Fame credentials primarily as a member of St. Louis's "Gashouse Gang," but he was acquired by Brooklyn during the 1940 season and went on to bat .318 with 18 homers and 88 RBI in '41. The Georgia-born Walker was one of the most outspoken opponents of the integration of baseball, but his on-field accomplishments earned him five straight all-star selections (1943–1947). In December 1947, Walker was traded to Pittsburgh in exchange for Billy Cox and Preacher Roe.

Duke Snider and Carl Furillo were stalwarts on the famed "Boys of Summer" of the 1950s. Both could hit and were phenoms in the outfield. Furillo was a typical Dodger—Italian American and salt of the earth—and was a fan favorite in Italian-heavy Brooklyn. He spent his entire career with the Dodgers, playing his final seasons in Los Angeles. Known as a tremendous fielder, Furillo also won a batting title in 1953 when he hit .344, and he accumulated more than 1,000 career RBI. Snider's combination of solid fielding and mighty bat earned him a place in Cooperstown.

Dixie Walker, 1946

Carl Furillo practices fielding fly balls at Ebbets Field, 1956

Willie Davis

Dusty Baker

The Dodger outfielders of the 1960s offered both speed and power. Wally Moon covered what there was of left field at the Coliseum in the late 1950s and early 1960s. He was succeeded by Tommy Davis, who might have gone down in history as one of the game's best hitters were it not for injuries. Davis was out of this world in 1962, batting .346 with 230 hits, 27 home runs, and a franchise-record 153 RBI. Willie Davis played center field from 1961 through 1973. He played basketball in school, but baseball scouts were enamored of his talents. Vin Scully said Davis worked as hard to become a center fielder as any player he ever observed, and the results were spectacular. He won Gold Glove awards, stole bases, and had decent home-run power. Frank Howard played alongside the two Davises from 1962 to 1964 and was the team's top home run hitter all three seasons.

Willie Crawford was another Los Angeles kid who roamed the vast Dodger Stadium plains. He played 10 games for the

Dodgers as a 17-year-old in 1964 and then stuck with the team until 1975.

Dusty Baker played alongside Hank Aaron in Atlanta before coming to the Dodgers in 1976, and he soon became a fan favorite in his eight seasons with the team. Baker's phenomenal play in the 1977 League Championship Series—.357 average and 8 RBI in 4 games—helped catapult the Dodgers to the World Series. His best season may have been 1981, when he won both the Gold Glove and Silver Slugger Awards. While Baker covered left field, the right field turf was handled by Reggie Smith from 1976 through 1981. The switch-hitting Smith was an MVP contender in 1977 by belting 32 homers and posting a league-high .427 on-base percentage.

Twenty-one-year-old outfielder Mike Marshall joined the Dodgers in 1981 when 38-year-old pitcher and former Dodger Mike Marshall was finishing up his career with the Mets.

Marshall the outfielder became a regular for LA in 1983 and helped lead the team to a division crown in 1985 with his 28 home runs and 95 RBI, both career highs. In 1988, veteran left fielder Kirk Gibson came to town and won the National League MVP. His 25 homers, .377 on-base percentage, and .483 slugging percentage were the high marks on the world championship squad.

When the hard-hitting, hard-throwing Raul Mondesi ended his seven-year tenure as the Dodgers' right fielder in 1999, in stepped Shawn Green. After hitting a respectable 24 homers in 2000, Green clubbed a combined 91 homers and 239 RBI during 2001 and 2002. Before moving to first base in 2004, Green missed a total of only seven games in four seasons.

Centerfielder Matt Kemp and right fielder Andre Ethier offer hope for the future in LA. They both hit for average and power, and Kemp brings speed to his repertoire as well. A relative veteran, Juan Pierre was the team's top base stealer in 2007 and 2008. The acquisition of Manny Ramirez in late July gave the Dodgers more depth, experience, and power to the outfield for their run for the division title in 2008.

Raul Mondesi

Juan Pierre, Andre Ethier, and Matt Kemp celebrate a Dodger victory, 2007

RIGHT-HANDED PITCHERS
From the Right

On the 1884 Brooklyn Atlantics, three pitchers accounted for ninety-nine percent of the innings pitched, and all three were right-handed. Nineteen-year-old Adonis Terry was the main workhorse, hurling 54 complete games and 476 innings. He struck out 230 batters—which stood as the franchise single-season record for 40 years—but posted a record of 19 wins and 35 losses. His fortunes improved over time, and in 1890, he went 26–16 for the NL-champion Bridegrooms. Bob Caruthers, Terry's teammate from 1888 to 1891, became the only 40-game winner in franchise history with his 40–11 mark in 1889.

Brooklyn's aces during the 1916 pennant season were righties Jeff Pfeffer and Larry Cheney, both of whom had ERAs of 1.92. Pfeffer's 2.31 ERA in eight seasons with Brooklyn is the best all-time among Dodger pitchers.

When baseball outlawed the spitball in 1920, Brooklyn's Burleigh Grimes was one of a handful of hurlers grandfathered in and allowed to continue the practice. He was 23–11 with a 2.22

Bob Caruthers, Old Judge & Gypsy Queen Cigarettes baseball card, 1888

Jeff Pfeffer

Burleigh Grimes

ERA for the 1920 pennant-winners, and he led the league with 22 wins the following year.

Dazzy Vance looked goofy, but his statistics do not. The Hall of Famer led the National League in strikeouts every year from 1922 to 1928. He didn't notch his first major league victory until the age of 31, in 1922, but he quickly made up for lost time. His 28–6 record in 1924 is the highest single-season win total by a Dodger pitcher after 1900. That year he was also tops in ERA (2.16), complete games (30), and strikeouts (262)—good enough to win the league MVP Award. He ranks among the franchise leaders in most career pitching stats.

While Clarence Arthur Vance was given a colorful nickname, Dazzy's colleague of the early 1930s didn't need one; his real name was colorful enough. Van Lingle Mungo joined the Dodgers in 1931 and remained with the team for a decade. A three-time all-star with Brooklyn, he regularly ranked among the league's strikeout leaders (he was tops in 1936 with 238) and won more than 100 games at a time when the team wasn't having much success.

Van Lingle Mungo

Dazzy Vance

Don Newcombe pitching, 1956 World Series

The Dodgers had a lot of success in the 1950s, and while hitting was the team's main calling card, several high-quality pitchers were integral to that success. A career Dodger, Carl Erskine had his best season in 1953, when he went 20–6. His best single-game performance was in Game Three of that year's World Series, when he set a postseason record with 14 strikeouts.

Don Newcombe won 20 or more games three times and, in 1956, captured both the Cy Young and MVP Awards on the strength of his 27–7 record. He was the first African-American pitcher to win 20 games. Despite missing two full seasons in his prime (1952 and 1953) while serving in the Korean War, Newcombe won 123 games as a Dodger, compared to Erskine's 122.

Don "Big D" Drysdale—a native of Los Angeles who attended Van Nuys High School with Robert Redford and Natalie Wood— had an impressive first full season for the Brooklyn Dodgers in 1957: 17–9 and 2.69 ERA. His statistics dipped a bit when the Dodgers moved into the hitter-friendly Los Angeles Memorial Coliseum, but Drysdale led the league in strikeouts in 1959 and

Dodger starting pitchers, 1952 (left to right): Joe Black, Carl Erskine, Preacher Roe, Billy Loes, and Johnny Rutherford

Don Drysdale pitching

1960. In 1962, the team's first season at Dodger Stadium, Drysdale won the Cy Young Award with a 25–9 record, 2.83 ERA, and 232 strikeouts. He finished with a 23–12 record and 2.77 ERA in 1965 despite playing with broken ribs for much of the stretch run. The 6-foot-6 Drysdale was an intimidating presence on the mound and was the league leader in hit batsmen five times. Forever linked with and sometimes overshadowed by teammate Sandy Koufax, Drysdale's 209 career wins, 2.95 lifetime ERA, and 2,486 career strikeouts rank him among the game's best—and he had to retire at the age of 32 because of arm injuries.

Rookie Don Drysdale gives Don Newcombe a hand with Newcombe's multiple awards, 1956

Don Sutton

Orel Hershiser

No pitcher won (or lost) more games for the Dodgers than Don Sutton. No Dodger pitcher struck out more batters than Sutton. And no Dodger in history threw more shutouts, started more games, or pitched more innings. Sutton started alongside Drysdale and Koufax as a rookie in 1966, and by 1972 he asserted himself as a star in his own right, finishing 19–9 with a 2.08 ERA and earning his first all-star selection. He won 21 games in 1976 and led the league in ERA in 1980, his final season in LA. Although he won more than 300 games and struck out more

than 3,500 batters in his major league career, Sutton never led the league in either category.

Orel Hershiser's numbers in 1985 were impressive—19–3 with a 2.03 ERA—but he ascended to another level of dominance in 1988. His 23–8 record helped carry the Dodgers to the world championship and earned Hershiser the Cy Young Award. He also won a Gold Glove Award and took home MVP honors for the National League Championship Series and World Series. Heading into the final game of the regular season, he was 10 innings short

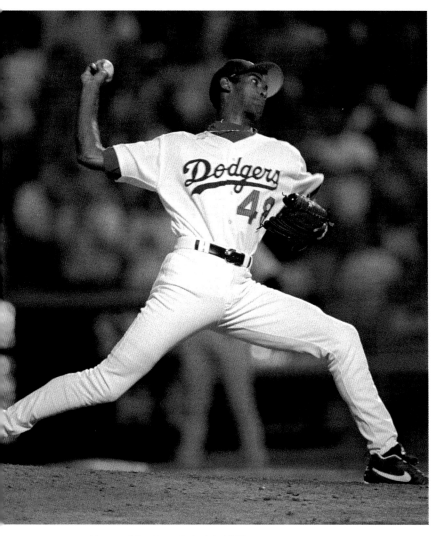

Ramon Martinez, July 14, 1995

Brad Penny, 2007

of breaking Drysdale's record for consecutive scoreless innings. As fate would have it, the game was tied 0–0 after nine innings, so Hershiser got to pitch an extra frame, put up a goose egg, and passed Drysdale with 59 shutout innings in a row.

Ramon Martinez is the last Dodger pitcher (as of 2008) to win 20 games in a season. His 20–6 mark in 1990 gave him all-star credentials, and on July 14, 1995, he became the sixth Los Angeles Dodger to pitch a no-hitter. The very next season, on September 17, 1996, Hideo Nomo threw a no-hitter in Colorado.

Nomo was a sensation for the Dodgers in the mid-1990s, striking out more than 230 batters every season from 1995 to 1997.

Los Angeles acquired hard-throwing Brad Penny in a midseason trade in 2004, and by 2006 he was the starting pitcher in the All-Star Game. He led the National League with 16 wins that season and followed it with a 16–4 record in 2007. The Dodgers signed Derek Lowe to a big contract in 2005, and although he hasn't matched the 21-win season that he had with Boston in 2002, Lowe has been a steady winner alongside Penny.

LEFT-HANDED PITCHERS
Southpaws

In the late 1800s, left-handed pitchers were a rarity in baseball. George "Nap" Rucker, the team's first southpaw ace, joined the Superbas in 1907 and spent his entire career with Brooklyn. His best season was 1911, when he sported a 22–18 mark. He retired in 1916 with a record of 134–134.

Former Giant Rube Marquard helped Brooklyn capture a pennant in 1916 by winning 13 games and posting a 1.58 ERA—the lowest mark in franchise history—and he won 19 games in 1917. After the 1920 season, Marquard was traded to Cincinnati for another lefty, Dutch Reuther, who led Brooklyn with 21 wins in 1922.

Watty Clark was nicknamed "Lefty" while playing for the "Daffiness Boys," and he was the team's winningest pitcher three times between 1929 and 1932. Following Clark's 20–12 season in 1932, it would be three decades before another Dodger lefty won 20 games in a season. Preacher Roe's 22–3 record in 1951 helped the Dodgers come oh-so-close to a pennant. Roe was chosen for the all-star team every year from 1949 to 1952, although his only action was a single inning in 1949.

Johnny Podres finished the 1955 season with a 9–10 record, but on a staff that included Don Newcombe, Carl Erskine, and Clem Labine, manager Walter Alston entrusted the 23-year-old Podres with the starting assignment in Game Seven of the World Series. The result: a complete-game shutout. Podres would go on to win 109 more games in a Dodger uniform, including an 18–5 season in 1961—but none was more significant than that 2–0 victory at Yankee Stadium on October 4, 1955.

Nap Rucker, 1915

Dutch Reuther, 1922

Preacher Roe

Johnny Podres, Game Seven, 1955 World Series

Sandy Koufax, 1965 World Series   *Claude Osteen, 1965 World Series*

The question of who was the greatest pitcher of all time can fuel barroom banter for hours, but it's nearly impossible to find a pitcher who dominated like Sandy Koufax did in the five-year span from 1962 to 1966. Three times during that stretch he had ERAs under 2.00, with a low of 1.73 in 1966. In 1963, '65, and '66—all three Cy Young seasons—he won 25 or more games and struck out more than 300 batters, including a then-major-league-record 382 in 1965. His 1962 and 1964 campaigns were cut short by injuries, but he still led the way in ERA both years and finished among the league leaders in strikeouts and winning percentage.

A healthy "Dandy Sandy" had a league-best 25 wins, 1.88 ERA, 11 shutouts, and 306 strikeouts in 1963. Winner of the MVP and Cy Young Awards, he absolutely dominated the Yankees in the opening game of LA's series sweep, leading Yogi Berra to wonder aloud how Koufax managed to lose even 5 games that year. In 1965, Koufax pitched his fourth no-hitter—a perfect game—and led the league in virtually everything (26–8, 2.04 ERA). In 1966,

he managed to be even better (27–9, 1.73 ERA), before hanging up the spikes at the top of his game because of severe arthritis in his arm.

Lefty Claude Osteen came to Los Angeles in 1965 and twice won 20 games for the Dodgers (1969, 1972). Osteen started at least 35 games every year from 1965 through 1971 and ranks seventh on the franchise victory list.

At 6-foot-5 and 200-plus pounds, Jerry Reuss was a prototype big-league pitcher. He won 18 games for Los Angeles twice and threw a no-hitter in 1980. Another southpaw of the era, Fernando Valenzuela, burst on the scene in 1981 (13–7, 2.48) and captured both the Cy Young and Rookie of the Year Awards. Valenzuela posted career highs with 21 wins and 242 strikeouts in 1986, but went 42–48 in his final four seasons with the Dodgers.

After Valenzuela, the Dodgers have not had another truly dominating lefty in the rotation. Odalis Perez won 15 games with a 3.00 ERA in 2002, and Kaz Ishii chipped in with 14 wins.

Jerry Reuss, 1981 World Series

Odalis Perez, 2002

Fernando Valenzuela, 1981

RELIEF PITCHERS
The Last Act

Closers are a relatively recent phenomenon. In the early days of baseball, a team's bullpen typically consisted of washouts or guys not good enough to start. If a man was pitching well, he was given the chance to finish the game. Occasionally, the team's ace would be called upon to mop up somebody else's mess. Nap Rucker started 33 games and finished 14 others in his 22-win season of 1911. Manager Wilbert Robinson used Rube Marquard in a similar fashion. Marquard started 20 games for the 1916 Robins and finished 11 more out of the bullpen. His five saves, to go along with 13 wins, helped make the difference in Brooklyn beating out Philadelphia for the pennant.

Al Mamaux was one of Brooklyn's first true relief specialists. From 1920 to 1923, he appeared in 95 games for the Robins but started only 27. One-time 20-game winner Jack Quinn started just 1 of his 39 games with the Dodgers in 1931 and had a league-high 15 saves.

The spitball-throwing Hugh Casey won 15 games for Brooklyn in 1939. As his number of starts declined, his saves increased. He led the league in 1942 and 1947, and averaged just 1⅔ innings per appearance in 1947.

Until 1989, no Dodger pitcher saved more games in a season than Jim Hughes did in 1954. (Jim Brewer tied his mark of 24 in 1970.) Clem Labine was the primary closer for the "Boys of Summer" during the decade. He led the league in saves in 1956 and 1957, and during the 1955 championship season, Labine pitched in relief in 52 games and notched 7 saves to go with his 11–6 record.

The Dodgers of the early 1960s used a committee of closers, led by burly southpaw Ron Perranoski. In 1962, Perranoski had 20 saves and finished 39 games, Larry Sherry had 11 saves and 26 games finished, and Ed Roebuck chipped in 9 saves and 22 games finished. Sherry, a product of Los Angeles' Fairfax High School, made his mark during the 1959 World Series, when he saved two games and won two others in relief against the White Sox, earning Series MVP honors. In 1966, Phil Regan was called "the Vulture" because he blew a number of leads only to have his team score to give him credit for the win; he went 14–1 and had 21 saves.

Nap Rucker, Turkey Red Cigarettes baseball card, 1911

Hugh Casey

Clem Labine

Ron Perranoski

Larry Sherry (left), with Duke Snider, 1959 World Series

Veteran Mike Marshall came to the Dodgers in 1974 insisting that he needed to pitch more and had found the antidote to arm injuries and stiffness. Manager Walt Alston allowed him to put his money where his mouth was. Marshall pitched and pitched and pitched, even when a game wasn't close. He appeared in a record 106 games in 1974 and finished with a 15–12 record, 21 saves, and a 2.42 earned run average in 208 innings. He was the first reliever ever to win the Cy Young Award.

Jay Howell helped LA capture the 1988 championship, and the following season he saved a then-franchise-record 28 games. Todd Worrell was the team's top closer in the 1990s and saved 44 games in 1995.

Mike Marshall, circa 1974

Todd Worrell, 1997

Eric Gagne is the only Dodger to top Worrell's single-season saves mark, and he did it three years in a row. After saving 52 games in 2002, he was even better in 2003, and nearly untouchable out of the bullpen. The Montreal-born righty saved 55 games with a 1.20 earned run average and earned Cy Young honors. He saved a record 84 straight games with no blown opportunities.

Japanese-born Takashi Saito took over the closer's role in 2006 and has been solid in his first three seasons in the United States. In 2007, he had 39 saves and a 1.40 ERA, and he added 17 more in 2008 while sharing closing duties with Jonathan Broxton, who saved 14 games for the West Division champs.

Eric Gagne, 2003

Takashi Saito, 2008

THE UNIFORMS
Dodger Blue

While some clubs seem to change their uniform styles and logo designs on an almost annual basis, the Dodgers have maintained a relatively consistent look to their attire for several decades. Earlier in the franchise's history, however, the uniforms adopted some more adventurous variations.

Collared shirts with button-down fronts and colored solid white or gray were the norm during the first decade of the twentieth century. Collars disappeared from the jerseys by 1910, and for a few seasons, a vertical strip featuring the word "Brooklyn" ran vertically over the buttons on road uniforms. Pinstripes as well as crisscrossing stripes, generally blue in color (red stripes appeared briefly in 1915), were experimented with at various times into the 1930s. By 1940, solid white and solid gray, occasionally tinted with

"Kid" Elberfeld, 1914

Elmer Stricklett, 1906

blue, became the standard. Zippers took the place of buttons on jerseys for a few seasons in the 1940s.

The lettering and logo has also remained largely the same since before World War II. In the early 1900s, the word "Brooklyn" was emblazoned in simple block letters across the front of road uniforms, and an ornate "B" insignia was placed on the left breast of home jerseys. The "B" was used both home and away for a period, and the insignia sometimes moved to the sleeve rather than the breast. Sometimes, there was no lettering or insignias at all.

The spelling out of "Dodgers" or "Brooklyn" reappeared on jerseys in the 1930s, using a serif typeface before the emergence

Sherry Smith, 1916

Ralph Branca, circa 1950

Brad Penny, 2007

Fernando Valenzuela, 1980s

of the now-familiar script lettering in about 1938. Road uniforms have displayed either the team name or the city (first "Brooklyn" then "Los Angeles") in the same type style for nearly 70 years.

Other than the temporary addition of trim or patches or other ornamentation—and the switch from wool or flannel material to doubleknit fabrics in the 1970s—the Dodgers of today are dressed in much the same style as the Dodgers of generations past.

Union Grounds, 1865

THE BALLPARKS
Home Games

Baseball had been played in Brooklyn as early as the 1850s on fields that were little more than open spaces with roughly defined boundaries. When William Cammeyer built a fence around his Union Grounds in the Williamsburg section of Brooklyn in 1862, the era of the enclosed ballpark—and, consequently, admission fees—was born. Union Grounds and the nearby Capitoline Grounds were used for various professional and semi-professional teams through the early 1880s.

The first home of the Dodgers' direct ancestors, the Atlantics of the American Association, was Washington Park, located in the Park Slope neighborhood of Brooklyn, in 1884. A fire in 1889 damaged much of the grandstand, and the ballpark was largely rebuilt. The team remained at Washington Park until 1891, when it split time between Washington Park and Eastern Park before making the latter its full-time home in 1892. Dissatisfied with the relatively remote location of Eastern Park, owner Charles Ebbets built a new ballpark near the old Washington

Eastern Park, circa 1894

Washington Park I, circa 1887

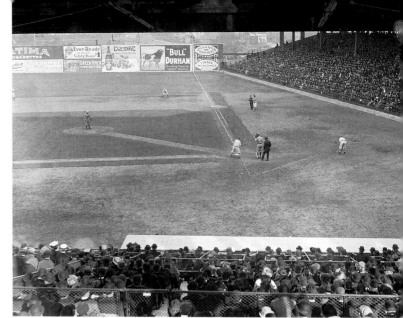

Opening exhibition game at Ebbets Field, April 5, 1913

Park site and gave it the same name of the previous park. The new Washington Park, which opened in 1898, featured a large grandstand that accommodated some 15,000 fans. There were no bleachers in right field, but a tenement building offered a view of the action. In left field, a chain-link fence separated bleacher seats from the field of play.

As the team struggled to draw heavy attendance during 15 seasons at Washington Park, Charles Ebbets was buying up plots for a new ballpark site in the Bedford-Stuyvesant section of Flatbush. By 1912, Ebbets had gotten enough property owners to sell, and construction of a new ballpark began.

Built of steel and concrete to better resist the ravages of fire, Ebbets Field featured an ornate brick exterior façade reminiscent of Manhattan's famed Flatiron Building, with office windows facing out of a curved structure. The ballpark's grand entrance rotunda was graced with Italian marble and featured a baseball-themed chandelier. As was typical of ballparks of the era, the dimensions of the playing field were dictated by the contours of the surrounding neighborhood, which made for some unique characteristics. The dominating characteristic of Ebbets Field, however, was its intimate atmosphere, which fostered a cozy, neighborhood feel for the thousands of fans that came out to see their beloved Dodgers.

Postcard view of Ebbets Field

When Walter O'Malley relocated the Dodgers from Brooklyn to Los Angeles in 1958, the team moved into one of the most bizarre, and arguably ill-suited, facilities in which major league baseball has been played. Although the Los Angeles Memorial Coliseum was legendary as the home of two major college football teams and site of the 1932 Summer Olympics, its four seasons hosting baseball (1958–1961) were most renowned for its odd field configuration and record-breaking attendance numbers. When O'Malley's new stadium in Chavez Ravine was finally completed in 1962, the Dodgers left the Coliseum and never looked back—at least not until 2008, when the team returned to the stadium for a preseason exhibition against the Boston Red Sox, which drew a world-record crowd of 115,300 fans.

When it opened on April 10, 1962, Dodger Stadium was considered the finest of baseball parks, and nearly half a century later, it still stands as one of the grandest facilities in the world. It was forged out of Chavez Ravine, a semi-abandoned plateau on a hill overlooking downtown LA. It was built to accommodate the car culture of the city, with acres of parking space and easy freeway access, centrally located from all areas of the Los Angeles Basin.

One of the last games at Ebbets Field, September 22, 1957

Secretary in the Dodgers office displays model for Dodger Stadium,
August 1960

First game at Dodger Stadium, April 10, 1962

Aerial view of Ebbets Field, circa 1950

Dodger Stadium is adorned with palm trees and foliage resembling the Hanging Gardens of Babylon, and indeed its grandiose presentation, combined with celebrity sightings that are endemic to its Los Angeles location, make the fan experience not unlike that of visiting a Cecil B. DeMille movie set. All 56,000 seats are angled to face home plate, with no pillars or posts blocking anybody's view, and it is the rare ballpark that has maintained the same seating capacity since the day it opened. It was also one of the last ballparks built entirely with private funds.

Although O'Malley and the City of Los Angeles faced bitter resistance from many residents of Chavez Ravine who were unwilling to sell their properties, the Dodgers ultimately prevailed. Upon opening in 1962, the stadium immediately began attracting record numbers of fans, thus validating Walter O'Malley's decision to move the team to Los Angeles.

Aerial view of Los Angeles Memorial Coliseum, 1959 World Series

Aerial view of Dodger Stadium, circa 1970s

OUTFIELD CONFIGURATIONS
The Outer Dimensions

The original Washington Park was used during the deadest of the dead-ball era, and outfielders stood some 50 feet from the "warning track." The only "fence" was human in nature: overflow crowds of fans, usually dressed to the nines, peering over one another to view the action. When Charles Ebbets built his new and improved Washington Park in 1898, the playing field was still rather vast, with a wooden fence sitting some 500 feet from home plate in deepest left-center field; suffice it to say, inside-the-park homers were a bit more common than the over-the-fence variety in those days. The dimensions were eventually reined in, and the final dimensions of Washington Park were about 300 feet down the foul lines and 400 feet to straightaway center.

Ebbets Field was the classic urban ballpark shoehorned into its site by surrounding streets and trolley lines. The right field wall was, at most, 301 feet from home, while left and center were originally 400 and 450 feet away, respectively. As grandstand and bleacher seating was expanded around the outfield, the dimensions of the playing field shrunk, and the intimate atmosphere within the park was heightened. By the time the Dodgers won their long-awaited championship in 1955, the dimensions were about 348 feet to left field, 393 feet to center, and 297 to right field—very enticing distances for the likes of sluggers Duke Snider, Gil Hodges, and Roy Campanella.

The Los Angeles Coliseum was a football field by design, and when it was retrofitted to accommodate baseball, the resulting dimensions were strange, to say the least. The left-field fence stood a mere 250 feet down the line from home plate. A 40-foot-tall screen built atop the fence reduced searing line-drives to doubles or singles. A looping pop-up, however, was good enough for a four-bagger, and outfielder Wally Moon took advantage with his "moon-shot" homers. Center field, which originally measured in at 440 feet from home, was gradually reduced to a mere 380.

Dodger Stadium was a pitcher's park, with uniform distances around the outfield and fences set far into the smoggy night: 330 feet down the foul lines and originally 410 feet to center field. The pitcher-friendly nature of Dodger Stadium was a reaction to the crazy Coliseum, but it helped to reinforce the team's emphasis on pitching and speed.

Washington Park, circa 1904

Ebbets Field, 1954

Dodger Stadium, 2007

Washington Park, 1911

BILLBOARDS AND SCOREBOARDS
Board Games

When it first opened, Brooklyn's Washington Park had no outfield walls on which to sell advertising, but once wooden fences were constructed, it became a prime spot for companies to hawk their wares. Attending a baseball game in Brooklyn at the turn of the last century apparently was not a family affair, as billboards in the outfield extolled the virtues of the seven deadly sins: Turkish Trophy cigarettes, Coronet Dry Gin, Imperial Beer, Philip Morris Cigarettes, Fatima Cigarettes, Green River Whiskey, Old Bushmill's Irish Whiskey, and B.V.D. undergarments.

Ebbets Field was a grand ballpark from the outside, and inside, some of the ballpark's most distinctive features were found in the outfield walls. The giant 40-foot scoreboard, installed in 1931, towered in right-center field. It was set within a concave wall that angled at a slight diagonal in the bottom portion. The oddly shaped wall and various nooks and crannies of the outfield

proved a challenge for visiting outfielders while being mastered by Brooklyn's own Duke Snider and Carl Furillo.

Set below the scoreboard was the iconic Abe Stark ad, which proclaimed "hit sign, win suit." Other familiar advertisements at Ebbets included those for Bulova watches, Gem razors, and Botany Ties. The large, illuminated Schaefer beer sign atop the scoreboard was one of many areas of dispute between team co-owners Branch Rickey and Walter O'Malley. The devout Rickey eschewed the old signs for strong drink and tobacco, but O'Malley saw money in the ads. Schaefer beer was popular, and the billboard paid well. Shortly after the sign went up, Rickey was gone. More than just an advertisement, the Schaefer sign was also part of the official scoring: the "h" in the word would light up to indicate a hit while an illuminated "e" signaled an error.

The Los Angeles Coliseum was unusual in nearly every way, not least of all the scoreboard. Located in one end zone of the football stadium, the scoreboard was in deepest center field when

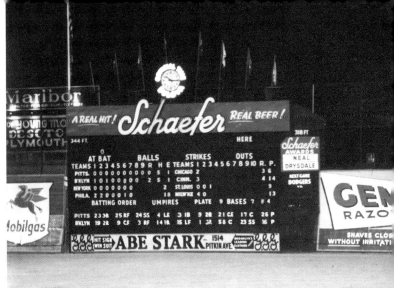

*Los Angeles Memorial Coliseum, Dodgers-Red Sox Exhibition,
March 2008*

Ebbets Field, 1957

the field was configured for baseball—about 800 feet from home plate. The scoreboard was almost closer to the Hollywood sign than to the catcher's signs.

Among Dodger Stadium's modern amenities were revolutionary twin scoreboards, one located on the left-field side for player information and announcements and one on the right-field side featuring vital statistics such as inning-by-inning runs, hits, errors, and pitch counts. These two scoreboards are still in place at Dodger Stadium with remarkably few variations, and neither one looks particularly outdated, which is a tribute to the modern-yet-traditional architectural philosophy employed in the Dodger Stadium design. The left-field board has been updated to include videos and animation.

The Dodgers have never given in to the temptation of selling corporate rights for the ballpark name, and the same resistance to outright commercialism is also evident inside the stadium. On the outfield walls, signs for banks and phone companies share space with paeans to past Dodger heroes. Electronic billboards were recently installed within the walls to provide both game details and advertising revenue.

*Dodger Stadium,
2005*

BULLPENS, DUGOUTS, AND CLUBHOUSES
All the Comforts of Home

One of the biggest changes in ballparks of today, compared to a century ago, is the improvement in the players' facilities, both on the field and behind the scenes. In the earliest days of baseball, dugouts were simply a bench set on the sidelines, with bats and other equipment strewn about. Clubhouses, where there were any, amounted to little more than concrete rooms with nails on the wall and meager shower facilities. And pitchers wanting to loosen up before a game simply stood off to the side of the diamond.

The steel-and-concrete Ebbets Field featured permanent dugouts with wooden benches—not exactly the epitome of comfort, but better than nothing. Bat racks and cubbies provided

Ebbets Field locker room, 1956

Dodger players in the Ebbets Field dugout, May 1955

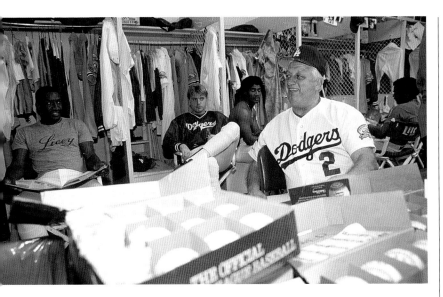

Dodger Stadium locker room, 1987

places to keep equipment stowed. The home clubhouse at Ebbets Field was located right next to the visitors' clubhouse When the Dodgers swept the Giants in August 1951 to extend their lead in the standings, the Giants could hear them whooping it up through the thin walls. According to legend, New York manager Leo Durocher used this event to fire up his team for the stretch run.

Dodger Stadium further modernized the dugout and clubhouse facilities for the players, though some are surprised to find that the home clubhouse is actually relatively small. The bullpens at Dodger Stadium were the first to be located beyond the outfield fences, instead of being part of the playing field. This not only provides the pitchers with a quiet sanctum in which to warm up, but also means that premier seating could be set closer to the playing field along the foul lines.

Dodger players celebrate Russell Martin's home run, August 2007

DODGER FANS

Bleeding Dodger Blue

odger fans have always been among the most loyal and enthusiastic in all of sports. While they have been criticized for their laid-back style in Los Angeles and a tendency to leave early to beat traffic, the consistent record-breaking attendance at the Coliseum and Dodger Stadium is proof positive that the Dodgers have a truly loyal fan base in LA.

Baseball fans in turn-of-the-century Brooklyn didn't have to fight freeway traffic, but they did have to look out for the speeding trolley cars that ran near the ballpark. The fans consequently came to be known as "trolley dodgers," providing the origin of the team's later nickname.

The fans at Ebbets Field enthusiastically supported their team through thick and thin, and the crowd featured colorful characters that became almost as well known as the players. The Dodgers Sym-phony was a makeshift band that provided

Fans at Ebbets Field showing their support, 1941

musical accompaniment, whether celebrating Dodger triumphs or mocking the opposition. Emmett Kelly, the team mascot, entertained the crowds while dressed in a clown costume evoking the "Bums" character that represented the Dodger fortunes over the years.

Although capacity at Ebbets Field was only 32,000 at its peak, the team's success on the field and resultant popularity meant that the Dodgers led the National League in attendance 10 times between 1940 and 1952. For a while, they were the hottest thing going in Brooklyn.

When the team relocated to California and set up shop in a converted football stadium, some people questioned whether baseball on the West Coast would make it. As it turned out, the fans couldn't get enough of the Dodgers at Los Angeles Coliseum, and in 1959, they became the first National League team to draw more than two million fans in a season. In May of that year, the Dodgers held "Roy Campanella Night" to honor the recently

Enthusiastic fans at Ebbets Field, 1947 World Series

paralyzed and much-beloved Dodger catcher. A record 93,103 showed up for the emotional event. When Pee Wee Reese wheeled Campy onto the field, the lights dimmed and tens of thousands of fans hoisted their lighters in a gloriously spiritual scene.

Dodger Stadium was built to accommodate 56,000 fans, and it has never been expanded despite the fact that sellout crowds have been the norm for years. The NL attendance leader in each of its first five seasons at the new stadium, the Dodgers attracted more than three million fans for the first time in 1978, a plateau they have reached more than 20 times since. And to illustrate that the enthusiasm is not waning, the franchise attendance record was set in 2007, when more than 3.8 million turned out to see the Dodgers.

Right: *Record crowd at preseason exhibition game, Los Angeles Memorial Coliseum, March 2008*

Angel Berroa celebrates with fans after winning West Division title, September 2008

Fans lined up outside Ebbets Field ticket office, 1952 World Series

The legions of fans that have come out to cheer on the Dodgers on both coasts over the decades have included a fair share of A-list celebrities. The stars of Broadway's Great White Way gravitated to winners, and until the 1940s, New York's winners were the Giants and Yankees. When the Dodgers started winning, the celebrities started coming to Ebbets Field in greater numbers. Manager Leo Durocher became friends with Frank Sinatra, who remained an avid Dodger booster in Los Angeles. Leo the Lip also befriended people on the periphery of organized crime and gambling rackets, among them actor George Raft.

At Ebbets Field, some of the more creative fans became celebrities in their own right. "Howling" Hilda Chester, with her clanging cowbells and loud cheers, would even heckle the Dodger players on occasion, but love her or hate her, everyone was familiar with this enthusiastic fan.

Danny Kaye grew up in Brooklyn and was batty for the Dodgers. He was an established star by the time the club moved to Los Angeles, and he became a regular at Dodger Stadium. In the late 1950s, then-actor Ronald Reagan helped spur approval of a city referendum to support building Dodger Stadium when he appeared on a telethon.

Cary Grant, the erudite Englishman, took to all things American, including baseball. He often sat with general manager Buzzie Bavasi and was far more than a casual fan. Doris Day

Fans lined up outside Washington Park ticket office, Opening Day 1908

was also a regular at Dodger Stadium and was rumored to have carried on a secret affair with Maury Wills.

Celebrity softball games became popular events at Dodger Stadium, with stars like Dean Martin participating, but what drew the most attention were beautiful women like *Playboy* model Barbi Benton. Dodgers players over the years have dated actresses, models, and singers. Celebrities of all statures come out to cheer on the team at Dodger Stadium. People-watching and star-gazing are favorite stadium activities, but without the paparazzi frenzy.

Actor Tom Hanks and family at Dodger Stadium, September 2004

Left: *Danny Kaye enjoying a hot dog at Dodger Stadium, early 1960s*

Fans lined up outside Dodger Stadium for playoff tickets, September 2004

FOOD AT THE BALLPARK

"Buy Me Some Peanuts and Cracker Jack"

Naturally, the best hot dogs in baseball were sold in and around Ebbets Field. After all, Brooklyn was the home of the famed Coney Island hot dog. Kosher hot dogs preferred by the borough's Jewish population were said to be so good because they "had to answer to a higher authority."

The popular Schaefer beer billboard in Brooklyn indicated fans' love for brew, which was an art form at the ballparks, taverns, and living rooms of its denizens. With a large Irish and Italian Catholic population, it was not uncommon to see friendly priests quaffing cold ones in Brooklyn.

Rod Dedeaux, who was briefly a Dodger and a longtime drinking buddy of Casey Stengel's, famously said, "No drinking before the game, but afterwards there's nothing like a tub o' suds." Dodger players were known to stop and join fans for a drink at the local pubs after games. Some would pick up a hot dog and cold beer outside the park on their way home. There was little hint of the velvet-rope treatment that separates today's players from their supporters.

Los Angeles' Dodger Dogs are legendary: long, thin hot dogs, lightly barbecued and served on fresh grilled buns. Generations of kids have fallen in love with them. Other popular treats for previous eras of Dodger fans included Walt's Malts and Dandy Sandy's ice cream. Vendor Roger Owens, who has been selling peanuts at Dodger Stadium since it opened, is a legend in his own right. He hurls bags of peanuts to customers halfway across seating

Fans buying hot dogs prior to the World Series at Ebbets Field, October 1920

Fan carrying hot dogs, nachos, peanuts, and soda at Dodger Stadium, May 2007

Two young fans enjoy Dodger Dogs and sodas at Dodger Stadium, May 2007

Peanut vendor, Dodger Stadium, circa 1980

sections with remarkable accuracy. His ability to hit his target is so uncanny that it seems the man could actually pitch in "the Show" if pressed.

For years, Miller Brewing had the beer account at Dodger Stadium, and the corporate maneuverings by its competitors to break this stronghold are legendary in beer biz circles, although that monopoly has been broken. Over time, Dodger Stadium has kept up with the Joneses by expanding food and refreshment selections for an increasingly health-conscious and eclectic fan base. Sushi and tacos are now popular items for the multicultural Dodger supporters.

The stadium club has long allowed celebrities and the powerful to dine in comfort without being bothered by other fans. Offering an unrestricted view of the stadium and game, the club offers five-star quality food and a fabulous buffet. (Despite the excellent offerings at the stadium club and refreshment stands, the press box offers notoriously below-par food in crowded confines.)

SPORTSWRITERS AND BROADCASTERS
The Poets

lthough Charles Ebbets neglected to include a press box in the plans for his new ballpark in 1913 (one was quickly added after construction), the Dodgers have a long history of being covered by the great masters of the written form and spoken word. The fact that the team has played in the two media capitals of the world—New York and Los Angeles—only increased the magnitude of their reach.

In the first half of the twentieth century, the *Brooklyn Eagle* newspaper had a small-town flavor to it. Serving its Brooklyn readership above all else, the newspaper was provincial, but it supported the Dodgers and was a big part of the deep attachment between the team and its borough.

But in some ways, the *Eagle* played a role in pushing the Dodgers out of Brooklyn. By tying the Dodgers so strongly to the borough, the idea of a move to Queens—which had been the only location approved by building commissioner Robert Moses in response to O'Malley's demands for a new stadium—was unthinkable. Then, when a crime wave hit Brooklyn after World War II, the *Eagle* responded with screaming, sensationalistic headlines, which spurred "white flight" to Long Island and

Larry MacPhail with sportswriters in his office, Ebbets Field

CBS television camera crew and radio announcer, Ebbets Field broadcast booth, August 1947

brought declining attendance to Ebbets Field. The paper finally folded, and without the *Eagle* left to editorialize against O'Malley's planned move to LA, the road was paved to California.

Columnists such as Ring Lardner, Westbrook Pegler, Red Smith, and Grantland Rice wrote thousands of colorful words about the Dodgers over the years. After the Dodgers moved to Los Angeles, publisher Otis Chandler decided to turn the *Los Angeles Times*, which had long served as a conservative mouthpiece, into a world-class paper. He succeeded in large measure by creating the best sports section in the business. The headliner was the great Jim Murray, who was to the written word what Vin Scully is to the spoken word.

When radio became popular in the 1930s, Red Barber established himself as a revered voice of the game. He covered the Dodgers for radio and then television from 1939 to 1953, and he was on air for the first televised baseball game, played at Ebbets Field in August 1939. The Mississippi-born Barber was beloved by Brooklyn fans for his colorful catchphrases and folksy style. Along with Mel Allen, in 1978, he became the first broadcaster honored by the Baseball Hall of Fame with the Ford C. Frick Award.

Barber also gave Vin Scully his big break, first bringing him on for college football broadcasts and then mentoring him in the Dodgers' broadcast booth. Barber's cadence, as in his description of Cookie Lavagetto's hit to break up Bill Bevens' World Series no-hitter in 1947 ("here comes the tying run, and here comes the WINNING run!") also influenced Scully's style.

Born and raised in New York, Scully never displayed a strong accent. Scully's rhythm is simply poetic, lyrical. He is among the finest sports announcers of all time. For Dodger fans, he is the unquestioned king of all announcers and a master of his craft.

Red Barber, Ebbets Field broadcast booth

Vin Scully, Dodger Stadium broadcast booth, May 2008

Dodgers at spring training, Hot Springs, Arkansas, March 1912

SPRING TRAINING
Dodgertown

Baseball teams in the early twentieth century would often head South to train before each season in the warm weather. In the 1910s, the Dodgers went to Hot Springs, Arkansas, a notorious gambling hangout and home to the "Dixie Mafia." After the 1919 "Black Sox" scandal, the club moved to Clearwater, Florida, and maintained a steady presence there for a few decades.

When Jackie Robinson signed, Branch Rickey sent the team to Havana, Cuba, ostensibly to shield Jackie and other black players from the harsh reception they might receive in the South. As it turned out, the black players were nevertheless housed in substandard segregated housing, away from the rest of the team, even though the local Cuban population certainly had no objection to them.

Dodger players workout at spring training, Clearwater, Florida, circa 1934

Dodger players workout at spring training, Dodgertown, Vero Beach, Florida, February 2007

Branch Rickey liked to do things on the cheap. Visionary as he was, he skimped on expenses for spring training, often to the discomfort of players. He would schedule exhibitions for profit that sometimes were a hardship for the team. Co-owner O'Malley's desire to invest in an elite spring training facility for the team was yet another chapter in the Rickey-O'Malley divide.

The club eventually found a spring home in abandoned Navy barracks at Vero Beach, Florida. Vero was off the beaten path and would serve to minimize the prejudice that the black players might face. Acting out of caution, the black players usually did not bring their wives to spring training. Maury Wills complained to the press that there were no good accommodations for black women anywhere near Vero. This remark did not go over well with Walter O'Malley, who had hated Robinson for his outspoken civil rights record and was discomfited by the "new breed" of African-American players like Wills. Still, the remark helped spur O'Malley to turn Dodgertown into the finest, and most self-contained, spring training facility in the major leagues. Dodgertown had everything: complete baseball and training facilities, living quarters, swimming pool, tennis courts, a golf course, and a rec center.

For decades, Dodgertown was the gold standard by which all spring training facilities were judged, but time eroded its polish and purpose. The Dodgers wanted to maintain a Florida training facility in order to hold onto the old New York fan base, much of which had moved to Florida in retirement, but by the 2000s that demographic had changed. Also, Florida's Grapefruit League is fairly spread out, requiring long bus rides to other teams' ballparks. The Cactus League in Arizona, however, is centered mainly in the Phoenix area and close to the city's resorts, golf courses, and nightlife. Arizona's growing popularity as a tourist attraction and baseball hub every February and March, along with its relatively close proximity to the home base of Los Angeles, spurred the Dodgers to abandon Dodgertown. In 2009, the Dodgers said farewell to Florida and held spring training in Glendale, Arizona.

Final game at Holman Stadium at Dodgertown, Vero Beach, Florida, March 2008

THE MINOR LEAGUES

It's a Long Way to the Top

Nearly every innovative way of thinking, new approach to the game, or baseball invention seems to have a Dodger stamp to it. Breaking the color barrier, a baseball academy in Latin America, a self-contained spring training facility, night baseball, regular radio and television coverage, West Coast expansion, the great accoutrements of Dodger Stadium—all of these developments were either initiated by the Brooklyn/Los Angeles Dodgers or perfected by them.

The minor league farm system is another example. Invented by Branch Rickey during his time with the St. Louis Cardinals, the farm system was perfected by Rickey and the Dodgers. It was no accident that the Cardinals and Dodgers were the dominant National League teams of the 1940s, while the behind-the-times Giants slipped.

For years, many major league clubs had agreements, some more formal than others, with minor league teams. The New York Yankees and the San Francisco Seals had an arrangement of sorts, which resulted not just in Joe DiMaggio becoming a Yankee, but in many Seals starring in New York. The "curse" of the Chicago Cubs has nothing to do with a billy goat. Rather, it has to do with owner Phil Wrigley allowing the Los Angeles market to get away.

Branch Rickey checks out the list of minor league prospects at Spring Training, 1948

Jackie Robinson with the Montreal Royals, April 1946

Branch Rickey with a young pitching prospect, circa 1948

He arranged for the Cubs to train at Catalina Island and had a minor league team playing in a stadium named after him in Los Angeles, but when he abandoned it, he also lost the LA talent base that then flowed to his competitors.

Rickey formulated the concept of a "farm" system, which went beyond a simple contract with a minor league team to establish a thorough organizational structure for scouting, signing, and training players in Dodger methods. Starting at age 17 or 18, players moved up the ladder to the next rung in the system, until, by the time a young player was 21 or 22, he had survived a grueling, competitive process and was either ready for big league ball or not. Rickey likened it to Jesus' admonition that "many are called, few are chosen."

It was a daunting process, but for those "chosen few," by the time they found themselves in the promised land—Ebbets Field—they had a sense that they were worthy of big league status. Before the institution of the free-agent draft in 1965 and the ascent of collegiate baseball, there were not only rookie league, class-A, double-A, and triple-A clubs, but also class-D and class-C teams seemingly in every tiny rural town across America. Life in the minors was hard, the conditions were rugged, and the weather was often inhospitably hot and humid. For black players, it could be particularly daunting because the system has always had a strong southern flavor to it, but any small town from California to New York had its share of anti-black sentiment in the 1940s, 1950s, and into the 1960s.

The number of affiliate teams in the Dodger system fluctuated over the years. When Rickey joined the organization in 1943, there were just three affiliate teams: Montreal, New Orleans, and Durham. The peak was in 1948, when as many as 28 minor league teams had ties to the Dodgers. From Medford, Oregon, to Nashua, New Hampshire; from Trois-Rivières, Quebec, to Abilene, Texas, young men across the nation were being groomed by coaches to learn the Dodger Way. Of course, the vast majority of those youngsters were lucky if they even made it as far as the triple-A squads in Montreal and St. Paul, Minnesota.

By the 1960s, the number of minor league teams in the Dodger organization was brought down to the more modest five or six. And while the host cities seem to change nearly every year, continuity remains a part of the system. Tommy Lasorda managed at nearly every level of the Dodgers' farm system; the players on the great Dodger squads in the 1970s all played for him at Ogden and Spokane on some of the best minor league teams of all time.

The team has had a long relationship with Albuquerque, New Mexico. The Albuquerque Dukes were the Dodgers' triple-A affiliate from 1972 to 2000, and the Dukes were a model of minor league success for years. The thin New Mexico air made it difficult for pitchers, but once they arrived in LA, they discovered that curve balls crackled even more, and fly balls did not carry as far. In 2009, the Dodgers signed a deal with the Albuquerque Isotopes of the triple-A Pacific Coast League.

From Branch Rickey's dream of a well-developed training system, minor league baseball has evolved into big business, with beautiful stadiums, fancy promotions, record-setting attendance, and amenities that even compete with the big league clubs.

Raul Mondesi with the Albuquerque Dukes, 1992

Eric Gagne, during rehab assignment with the double-A Las Vegas 51s, May 2005

BIBLIOGRAPHY AND RESOURCES

Baseball Encyclopedia. New York: Macmillan, 1996.

Johnson, Steve. *Chicago Cubs Yesterday & Today*. Minneapolis: Voyageur Press, 2008.

Leventhal, Josh. *The World Series*. New York: Tess Press, 2004.

_____. *Baseball Yesterday and Today*. Minneapolis: Voyageur Press, 2006.

Los Angeles Dodgers 2001 Media Guide. Los Angeles: Los Angeles Dodgers, 2001.

Prince, Carl. *Brooklyn's Dodger*. New York: Oxford University Press, 1996.

Snider, Duke, with Phil Pepe. *Few and Chosen: Defining Dodger Greatness Across the Eras*. Chicago: Triumph Books, 2006.

Stout, Glenn. *The Dodgers: 120 Years of Dodgers Baseball*. New York: Houghton-Mifflin Co., 2004.

Travers, Steven. *Dodgers Essential: Everything You Need to Know to be a Real Fan!* Chicago: Triumph Books, 2007.

_____. *Angels Essential: Everything You Need to Know to be a Real Fan!* Chicago: Triumph Books, 2007.

Whittingham, Richard. *Illustrated History of the Dodgers*. Chicago: Triumph Books, 2005.

INDEX

ABOUT THE AUTHOR

STEVEN TRAVERS is a graduate of the University
of Southern California and an ex-professional
baseball player. He helped lead his suburban
California high school baseball team to the
national championship in his senior year;
attended college on an athletic scholarship; was
an all-conference pitcher; and coached at USC,
at Cal-Berkeley, and in Europe. He also attended
law school, served in the Army, was a sports
agent, and is a guest lecturer at the University
of Southern California. He is the author of
numerous books, including *Dodgers Essential:
Everything You Need to Know to Be a Real Fan!,
Barry Bonds: Baseball's Superman, The Good,
the Bad, and the Ugly Los Angeles Lakers, The*

USC Trojans: College Football's All-Time Greatest Dynasty, and *The 1969 Miracle Mets.* Steve
was a columnist for *StreetZebra* magazine in Los Angeles and the *San Francisco Examiner*
and has written for the *Los Angeles Times* and the *Los Angeles Daily News.* He also penned
the screenplay, *The Lost Battalion.* A fifth-generation Californian, Steve has a daughter,
Elizabeth Travers, and still resides in the Golden State.